By Design

Cloverton Romance Book Six

Haven Saunders with Marci Wilson

MaHanna Media, LLC

Copyright © 2024 by MaHanna Press, LLC

All rights reserved.

Cover: getcovers.com

No portion of this book may be reproduced in any form without written permission from the publisher or author, except as permitted by U.S. copyright law.

Chapter One

Thea Winton hated summer. She hated sweat. She hated mosquitoes. And most of all, she hated sunburns.

Which was quite a problem since she made her living working outdoors as a junior landscape architect. Tate Landscaping, the only business of its kind in the area, was a recent addition to the town of Cloverton. The business was an offshoot of their main office based in the Quad Cities in eastern Iowa.

Thea had started the previous year when the season was starting to crumple into fall and the world was temperate and exciting. This was her first full summer with Tate, and the heat was making her miserable.

So, when she arrived at the tiny French café that had recently opened, she surprised the hostess by asking for a table inside.

Thea ordered an Aperol spritz and then basked in the air conditioning. She didn't even care that Zoe Redford was nearly half an hour late. Being inside felt divine.

When Zoe finally arrived, the redhead bumbled in with her guitar case strapped to her back, barely missing hitting a passing server in the face with the headstock. "Sorry!"

Thea laughed and shook her head. Her best friend had always been a bit of a hot mess, but that seemed to be the case more often these days.

Zoe plopped into the chair with a heavy sigh. "I had to grab Ella from camp and take her to the restaurant, so I was late to my four-thirty lesson and—"

"Zoe, I promise, it's fine. I didn't even realize you were late." Thea was proud of her friend. Ever since returning to Cloverton, Zoe had taken up giving lessons to the locals and was also teaching summer music classes. Thea hoped it would lead to Zoe opening her own school.

Zoe smiled sheepishly. "Still." She got herself situated, took a deep breath, and sighed. "Okay. How was work?"

"I'm surprised you can't smell me from where you're sitting," Thea grumbled.

"Fresh as a daisy."

"Liar."

Zoe laughed. "I can't smell you, Thea."

"Well, I was sweating like a pig today. We're finishing up a job at the post office in Raidington."

Zoe rolled her eyes. "God, their *post office* needs *landscaping*? Our post office is literally a box with a parking lot."

"The Raidington Post Office now has a duck pond."

Zoe slammed her hands on the table. "No!"

"Yes!"

The two women threw their heads back in laughter like they used to when they were kids and were only interrupted by a server coming to take Zoe's drink order. Thea and Zoe had been the best of friends since they were babies. And though they grew up in different directions, their roots were always entangled. Thea was serious and focused while Zoe was dreamy and free-wheeling.

When Zoe had left Cloverton for California several years prior, Thea had been the one to ask if she was sure she wanted to do it. Moving to L.A. didn't seem practical to Thea. But Zoe had to follow her dreams, and Thea respected that.

Now that Zoe was back, Thea was thrilled.

"Anyway, I don't want to talk about work. Tomorrow is Friday and then we're done with it." Thea brushed her bobbed brown curls out of her face. "Let's talk about you."

Zoe flushed. "What about me?"

"I don't know. You're, like, a mom now."

"Stop it."

Thea gaped. "You are! You've basically got a kid."

Zoe looked down at her flatware, adjusting her fork absentmindedly. "I guess."

Though her friend was being coy, Thea knew that Zoe was thrilled with her new life. Within the first three months of the year, Zoe had returned home, met Marty Martinez—the owner of the local diner—and fallen madly in love with him and his six-year-old daughter. They were already living together.

To grounded, straitlaced Thea, it was all insane.

And yet, she couldn't help being a bit jealous. Thea hadn't left Cloverton like Zoe had. Even when she was in college, she lived with her parents and commuted. She'd never really left the bubble of the small town and, consequently, not much had happened to her. Sure, she got a degree and a new job.

But a relationship? Nothing of the kind.

Not for lack of trying. Thea was always trying out the latest app to meet her soulmate. She'd been on more first dates than she'd like to admit. However, none of them were the right fit. They either didn't light Thea's soul on fire, or they decided to disappear after a couple of weeks, sometimes months, of dating. Or talking. Thea couldn't tell what infuriated her more, summer or the *talking* phase.

Her mother thought she was too picky. "No one is perfect, Thea," her mom loved to remind her. "You need to let someone open up to you."

Yet, no matter how charming or funny or handsome her dates were, she felt nothing. Even the ones who ended up abandoning her were no real loss.

Thea was starting to think she was broken.

"I'm happy," Zoe said suddenly.

Thea frowned. "Of course you are."

"That's not what I ..." She took a deep breath. "I know you're worried that things are moving fast but it's right. You know?"

The cynic inside Thea couldn't believe Zoe. How could her friend just know? And know well enough to take such risks? Moving in with a man after a few weeks was insane enough, but a man with a child?

Only Zoe Redford.

"I wish I knew," Thea said softly.

Zoe smiled. "Didn't you have a date last night?"

Thea shook her head. "I mean, I did, but I cancelled."

"Thea!"

"What?"

"You're never going to meet anyone if you *cancel*."

"Do you know how many dates I've been on in the past three months?"

Zoe twisted her lips together. She knew very well how many people Thea had met. She'd run out of eligible men within a twenty-five-mile radius and was starting to drive nearly forty-five minutes away just to find someone who might be suitable. However, no matter what, Zoe never said Thea was too picky.

Thea was grateful for that.

"I'm tired, Zo. I'm really tired."

The server arrived with an Aperol spritz for Zoe and Thea quickly ordered another one for herself. Drinking wasn't the answer, but it certainly helped. "You're in your mid-twenties, Thea," Zoe said before taking a sip of the bubbly drink.

"So?"

"So, you have plenty of time."

In the scheme of the world, maybe. But something was happening in Cloverton. It seemed like everywhere she looked, people in the sleepy town were falling in love. This was another reason Thea hated summer. Everyone loped about with their love on display, hands interlaced, stealing kisses as they walked down Main Street.

Barf.

"I don't want more time. I want to find my person."

Zoe grunted. "Love isn't like that."

"Yes, it is. It's not as woo-woo, manifestation, soulmate, kindred spirit as people want us to believe," Thea replied with an edge to her voice. "It's objective. Find a partner. A good person. Who makes good money and has values that align with yours and goals that align with yours and—"

Zoe started laughing. "None of that is objective, Thea!"

"But it is. It's measurable. It's simple. And men don't want to make it simple."

"Oh, Thea."

"Don't 'oh, Thea' me."

Zoe couldn't hide how humorous she found her friend, even as she looked down at the menu. "Maybe you need to meet someone the old-fashioned way."

"How? Everyone is taken. Even Ginny DePowell managed to find someone while I'm—"

"Ginny deserves it."

"I'm not saying she doesn't deserve it. I'm saying that ..." What was Thea saying? That Ginny should be alone just to make her feel better? Even in her heightened state of emotion, she knew that was crazy. "All the eligible bachelors in Cloverton are no longer eligible. That's all."

Zoe folded her menu closed. "That's not true."

Thea raised an eyebrow. "If you're about to try and set me up with Will—"

Her friend's eyes bugged out at the mention of her high school ex-boyfriend and former fling. "No. I would never do that to you. Besides, you two would be horrible together."

Thea giggled.

"No, I think I have someone for you."

"Zoe."

Zoe held up her hand. "And it's not one of Marty's friends. I know you don't like older guys like I do."

Thea breathed a sigh of relief. "So, what are you saying, you're going to set me up?"

"Maybe."

"But?"

Zoe's gaze found Thea's. "You have to promise to go into it with an open mind. Like assuming the *best* of intentions. Okay?"

Why does that seem so hard? Though Thea's insides locked together at the idea of giving a man, any man, the benefit of the doubt, she nodded curtly. "All right. I will give him the benefit of the doubt."

"Okay."

"So who is it?"

Zoe cocked her head to the side. "One of my students."

"What's his name?"

"I'm not going to tell you."

"What?"

"I'm not telling you. Not until I talk to him first." Zoe looked very pleased with herself as her plan came together.

"You need to get out of that app dating culture and meet someone. See if you have chemistry before knowing his job or where he grew up or how tall he *says* he is."

Shaking her head, Thea groaned. "They always say they're five ten when they're only—"

"Five-eight, I know, you've said." Zoe eyed her friend. "And it's insane that you are judging men based on that before you know anything about them."

Thea's shoulders drooped. "I'm shallow, aren't I?"

Zoe grabbed Thea's hand. "That's not what I'm saying. You've been working with what you have. But I don't think what you have is *working*. Does that make sense?"

Thea was not the type to trust in the universe. She looked up menus at restaurants before she arrived, so she knew exactly what she was going to get. She made sure she had her keys and wallet three times before walking out the door. She even carried folded-up toilet paper in her purse on the off chance she used a stall without any.

Letting go was not in Thea's vocabulary.

"I'm going to text him now," Zoe said, whipping out her phone. "And see if he's free to take you out tomorrow."

"Tomorrow?"

"Tomorrow."

"Zoe, I can't tomorrow, I'm—"

"What?" her friend asked dryly, still staring at her phone. "Washing your hair?"

Thea swallowed. "You know taking care of my hair is a process."

Zoe smirked to herself and then put down the phone. "Sent."

"Oh *God*."

"Hey. Let's drink. And forget about it, okay?"

Thea took a deep breath. If she wanted anything to change, she had to *let* things change.

It didn't mean she had to be happy about it.

Putting the text into the back of their minds, the two women sipped their Aperols, ordered and ate delicious Parisian-inspired food, and chatted the night away until Zoe's phone buzzed loudly on the table.

Thea's heart dropped as she watched Zoe pick it up and check the text.

"Tomorrow. Seven-thirty. You have a date."

To Thea's surprise, the dread was replaced with a different feeling. Something she hadn't felt for a date in a long time.

Anticipation. Possibility.

Excitement.

"All right, then ..." Thea trailed off, deep in thought. "You have to help me pick out what to wear."

Zoe grinned. "Deal."

Chapter Two

Derek Harper was thrilled that today was the last day he would have to drive to Raidington. It was out of the way, the roads leading to the town were littered with potholes, and on more than one occasion he had been trapped by a train stopped on the tracks separating the backroads from his destination.

He was already a terminally unpunctual person. Now, Raidington made it worse.

And, it was a simple point of fact, everyone from Cloverton *hated* Raidington. They called it *Richington* which wasn't necessarily a clever nickname, but a fitting one. While Cloverton floundered in the years following the mill's closure, Raidington continued to thrive as a getaway destination for Chicago's semi-elite.

Derek was not a Cloverton native. In fact, he lived far on the outskirts of town. But he'd quickly found his place within the fold working at Tate's Landscaping and had assumed the native hatred of Raidington.

With his windows down and music booming through the speakers, Derek finally approached the Raidington post office in his big truck. The image would be dissonant to anyone. A prim post office with a duck pond and rolling beds of flowers versus the hard black edges and glinting chrome of his truck.

This brought Derek great pleasure.

The work site was already bustling with his coworkers, mostly young men who were putting the finishing touches on the lawn outside the post office. It had come together in the past several weeks with remarkable efficiency, especially considering they'd dug out the pond themselves.

Derek parked haphazardly and leaped out of his truck. He stripped his flannel shirt off and tied it around his waist. It was too hot for an overlayer. He'd sweat through his tank top in less than an hour anyway.

"Harper!"

Shit.

"You're late."

Derek turned to look at the source of the voice, the approaching stick-up-her-ass Thea Winton. "Thea. What's up? TGIF, am I right?"

Thea's stoic expression didn't change. She stopped in front of him, crossing her arms over her chest. "You said that you'd have the aerator working by noon."

"It's nine-thirty. I'll get it done," he said, trying to tamp down the annoyance in his voice.

Her lips curled, sour to his response.

Derek, however, did not feel any desire or need to make her feel any better. He had a job to do, and he'd get it done. All she had to do was get out of his way. "Okay, well, good morning to you too," he muttered before going to the back of the truck to get his tool belt.

Thea Winton had been a thorn in his side from the moment they'd started working together at Tate. The first moment he saw her, he thought she was stunning. Could have been a model even. Curly dark hair, gorgeous cheekbones, and full luscious lips, a pair of gray-blue eyes that looked like a hazy seascape. But after one day of working together, Derek could barely stand her. She was bossy, pretentious, and cold, while Derek was a wild goofball. They were like oil and water and had never, ever, been able to mix.

Yet he couldn't help his mind from lingering on the thought of her from time to time. Her iciness sometimes sparked something in him. The desire to prove himself to her and the notion that somehow, someday, he could earn her softness.

Then, she'd pull shit like this, and he'd be annoyed with her for the rest of the day.

And, in classic Thea fashion, she wasn't done. She followed him to the back of the truck like a puppy nipping at his heels. "This has to be perfect, Derek."

"Don't you have something to be doing, Thea? Other than hounding me?" He clipped his tool belt on.

"I'm in charge of the final walkthrough today, and I'm not going to have it be anything less than perfect."

"So Tim is having you do the grunt work, huh?" he asked drolly.

Thea opened her mouth. "I take umbrage with that description."

Derek chuckled to himself. "Okay."

They stared at each other. It was a shame Thea was such a pain in the ass. She was a pretty woman. But she was a perfectionist and a brown noser. She'd been cozying up to the boss, vying for some sort of promotion, since the very first week of working at Tate. Desperate to prove herself.

Derek couldn't understand people who lived to work. He worked to live. To pay his mortgage and help his family with bills. Being a landscaper and getting his hands dirty was nothing more than a conduit to being able to survive.

"If you don't have it done by noon, then the final trims are going to take longer. We'll have to stay late," Thea said matter-of-factly.

Derek shook his head. "Well, that's not going to happen."

"You can say that all you want—"

"No, Thea, I'm telling you, it's not going to happen. I've got plans. So even if for some reason something goes a little amiss in your book, I'm out of here at five," Derek said firmly and then strode off in the direction of the duck pond.

Still, Thea followed. "You know, that's not how this works."

"Are you promising me overtime? That's a different story."

"I didn't say that."

Derek stopped suddenly and turned back to look at Thea. "You know most of us have lives on a Friday night. We go home and forget about the work and try and enjoy ourselves. You should try it sometime."

Thea huffed softly. "It's not a bad thing that I care about my job."

Derek shook his head. "I can care about my job and not have it be my life."

"It's not my life."

"Okay, then what are *you* doing tonight, Thea?"

"I have plans, too, for your information."

Derek scoffed. "Really? What type of plans?"

Thea's cheek twitched. "Just. Plans."

He nodded slowly. "Totally. Plans. See. We both have plans. Both have places to be. Guess I should get to work so we can both get to our *plans*, Thea."

"I do have plans," she replied.

Derek backed away. "Not saying you don't."

"Well, it sounds like you are."

"It's kinda weird that you're not saying what your plans are. That's what makes me suspicious."

Thea opened her mouth and then put her hands on her hips. "You're not saying what your plans are."

"Is that what this is? An eye for an eye?"

She pursed her lips. "I don't know why I'm supposed to believe you blindly and you get to question me."

Derek smiled. "Well, forgive me, Thea, but I don't know you to be a person who has plans often."

"Just because I don't have plans often, doesn't mean—" She stopped and made a noise of frustration. "Whatever, I don't care if you believe me."

Their constant bickering was new. It started as passive aggression when Thea was just getting her footing as an underling of their boss, Tim. Slowly, but surely, she grew into her role, and, with it, came her bossiness. Now, barely a day went by when Derek and Thea didn't get into something. It certainly didn't help that Derek liked to rile her up. He relished watching her go red in the face and her forehead fold into deep wrinkles when he said something that made her cross.

"I have a date," he proffered kindly. *Let's bury this hatchet*, he thought. *For now.* "That's why I'm not going to be staying late. Happy?"

Derek didn't like to talk about his personal life if he could help it. Especially dating. He hadn't been on a date since his ex broke up with him three years ago. The wound had been deep. He'd already laid down more money than he should have on an engagement ring. The wound was so deep that he skipped town. Not too far away, only about an hour. He still needed to be close to his family.

He hated to say it, but finding Cloverton was kind of like finding himself. He'd grown up over the past few years. Spent a lot of time on himself. Buying a house, fixing it up, going to therapy, making new friends.

He'd avoided dating completely that whole time. It was time to get back out there and see if he could find someone to share everything with.

Thea was taken aback by his offer of information. "Oh. Okay. Well." She looked away. "I have a date too."

"Great. Now we know." That was quite enough for Derek. He wasn't interested in the poor sap who was going to have to sit across from Thea Winton and hang on to every word she said about the merits of landscape architecture. Or whatever else Thea liked to talk about.

With the conversation sufficiently over, Derek finally got away from Thea and went in the direction of a pile of cement blocks beside the duck pond he'd prepared the day before in order to create a mooring for the fountain. "Okay, let's do this."

He touched his wrist expecting there to be a hair tie waiting for him, but immediately realized he'd forgotten to slip one on this morning. *This is what you get for being late.*

Moments like this made him want to cut his hair. But he'd had it long all of his adult life. Since his sophomore year of high school. It was a way he could connect with his Native American heritage, one that had been squelched and assimilated out of the region. For the past twelve years, Derek had done everything he could to reexamine his family's Neshnabe heritage, or what people in the area knew better as *Potawatomi*.

Long hair was a symbolic tie with Mother Hearth. Power, virility, strength. And though it made him feel more rooted to his ancestors, it didn't mean it wasn't a pain in the ass.

"Here."

Derek turned to look over his shoulder, finding Thea had followed him once more. Except this time, it wasn't to nag him to death. Between her fingers, she held a thin hair tie.

"You sure?" he asked softly.

"Yeah. It's an extra."

Derek took it sheepishly, not feeling he truly deserved it after being so petulant with her a few minutes before. "Thank you."

Thea shrugged and then narrowed her eyes. "Noon, Harper."

And there went any impulse to feel bad for being mouthy to her. *Harper. Why does she treat me like I'm on a football team? She's not my coach. She's not even my boss. She's just ...*

Thea left, rushing off in the direction of the cobblestone walkway leading to the post office where several of the guys were scratching their heads over a limp patch of pink muhly grass.

Deep breath. Get it done.

Yes, to Derek, a job was just a job. However, he could have picked a worse one. He'd had the grades to go to a college in the city, and then get some sort of corporate job. Perhaps he'd have a condo downtown instead of a bungalow amidst the cornfields.

However, Derek valued the land. It's why he'd worked at the garden store and now with Tate's. He wasn't always able to do right by the land, what with fertilizer and uprooting trees and shrubs for no good reason. But most days, he could count on the satisfaction of kneeling in the grass and getting his hands dirty, connecting with the soil his ancestors had connected with years and years ago.

That made all the headaches of being pushed around by Thea Winton worth it. Most days.

Chapter Three

Thea tapped her fingers against the table, nervously watching the front door of the restaurant.

"I told him to wear a green tie," Zoe had explained. "You'll wear a green dress. That's how you'll know each other."

When she'd arrived at the restaurant, she told the host the silliness regarding her dress. "This is going to sound ridiculous, but I'm wearing green and meeting a guy here who is also going to be wearing green, so ... Can you send him my way if you see him?"

The host was more than eager to help out, to Thea's dismay. She almost would have rather the hostess be confused and cold about it rather than *excited*. Thinking she was playing some sort of part in a blossoming romance.

However ... maybe it was okay to be hopeful. Just a little bit.

Thea's heart skipped a beat every time the door opened. Every person, regardless of whether they were clearly alone or not, she'd check for the green tie. There had been only one disappointment in the bunch: a man who looked about thirty, wearing a handsome navy suit, his blonde hair dashingly tousled with product, and a suave smile on his face.

Of course he was quickly followed by his date for the evening. Someone as blonde and attractive as he was.

I bet they have terrible sex, Thea thought.

After about fifteen minutes, the server finally approached her. "Can I get you a drink while you're waiting?"

Why are people always keeping me waiting? "Um ..." Thea glanced at the door once more in case her suitor walked in right then and there. Nothing. "A bottle of red. A nice one." If he was going to keep her waiting, he was going to be treating her to a very nice dinner. "Two glasses, of course."

The server smiled. His white button down and black vest and bowtie hung off him like he was a scarecrow. "Right away, ma'am."

Ma'am? She wasn't old enough to be a ma'am. Was she?

Thea watched the server walk off, and then casually glanced back at the front door.

Her whole body froze with fear when she saw Derek Harper at the host stand.

You've got to be kidding me. He's having a date here, of all places? What are the fucking chances?

BY DESIGN   21

She stared a second longer than she should have because, well, he looked good. Derek didn't seem like the type to own a suit, yet there he was in a charcoal number that somehow made him look bigger than he already was. He was wearing his hair down over his shoulders, his jet-black lock flowing freely.

And the way he smiled at the hostess, bright white teeth standing out against his burnt umber skin. Fuck.

Thea grabbed the menu and propped it in front of her face. *Please don't see me. Please don't see me.* The only thing that could make this night worse was if Derek saw her here and had a firsthand account of how she met a stranger, and it went miserably.

God, that would be absolutely catastrophic.

As she hid behind the menu, Thea looked askance at the other tables. There wasn't a single woman alone. She wondered who he could be meeting.

"Are you the girl wearing green?"

Derek's voice.

Thea's stomach turned into a stone. *Why is he asking me if I'm wearing green? Unless ... No. No way. It can't be.*

"I'm nervous, too. It's okay. I don't bite, promise."

Thea slowly lowered the menu from in front of her face. "Hi, Derek."

She watched his nervous smile turn into a look of horror. "Thea?"

Her eyes fell on his chest. A dark green tie with pink flowers dotting the fabric. "You're the guy in the green tie?"

Derek grabbed his tie and looked down at it as if he couldn't believe it.

"Oh my God." Thea dropped her head into her hands. "This is awful."

"I don't look *that* bad."

"No, that's not what I—" Thea frowned. "You take guitar lessons with Zoe?"

Derek looked away. "Um. Yeah."

"Oh. I had no idea."

"It's not something I talk about because I'm not very good." He swallowed. "You're Zoe's best friend?"

"Yeah."

A smile crinkled onto his face. "That makes literally no sense at all."

"What's that supposed to mean?"

"Well, she's, like, a free-spirit and you're ... you."

Thea gasped incredulously. "Well, this has been great, but ..." She got to her feet and grabbed her clutch.

"Wait, I didn't mean it in a mean way."

She shook her head. She didn't care how he meant it. This night was already more mortifying than she possibly could have prepared for. "Don't worry about it. Let's just pretend this didn't happen, okay?"

"Thea, wait." Derek grabbed Thea's upper arm.

She'd never felt his touch, not even in so much as passing. Feeling his fingers pressing into her skin was electrifying.

"We both came all the way out here."

"Derek, I don't want to pretend like we ..." Thea was about to say 'like each other,' but there really was no reason for their mutual disdain other than work ethic. Overall, Derek seemed like a nice guy. Just wasn't someone she enjoyed working with. His attitude was cavalier and casual. Meanwhile, she liked things to run a very particular way, down to the minute if she could help it.

"I'm sorry to interrupt, but ..." The scrawny server returned, a bottle of wine in his hands like an offering.

Thea looked at the wine and then at Derek. He smiled, a small off-kilter smile. The subtext read, *Why not?*

And truly, why not? What was there to lose other than a couple of hours? Otherwise, she'd be heading right home to order some takeout to eat sadly in bed. "Yes, sorry. Um, let's sit."

Derek nodded, releasing her arm. Thea immediately felt an emptiness. *What the hell was that?*

They sat across from each other nervously as their server opened the bottle of wine and poured it for them. Neither dared to look at the other. When the server had gone, they were left in a well of silence.

"That's a nice bottle of wine," Derek remarked.

"You can tell?"

He shrugged. "I know a thing or two."

Thea didn't know the first thing about wine. That Derek could tell, based on the label, that she'd picked out something on the more expensive end was impressive. "Since you were late, I took the liberty of ordering something nice. Although, I didn't know it was going to be you, so ..."

"I get it."

Thea sipped her wine carefully and then sighed. "This is so weird."

"So weird."

They both looked at one another. And then, suddenly, were laughing. The abject absurdity of the situation hit them at once, leaving them in stitches.

"You're my blind date," Thea said, trying to come to grips with her reality.

"I know, it's crazy."

She took another gulp of wine. "Well, don't feel compelled to keep it a date."

"Oh, no, definitely not. You either."

That stung just enough to knock Thea off balance. Why wouldn't he want to be on a date with her? All their rivalry aside. Surely, she was a catch, right?

"Even if there was something here, we couldn't ... you know."

"Right, and there isn't, so ..."

"Yes, exactly."

Dating at Tate was a strict no-no. An HR nightmare. A cause for firing. It was an intense policy, but Thea had never questioned it.

Until now.

"Look, this is maybe a good thing," Derek said carefully. "I don't know if you feel that there's a gap between us, but ..."

"I do. Yeah. I feel that."

He swallowed. Thea's eyes immediately fixated on his protruding Adam's apple. *Oh my God. Am I attracted to*

Derek? "Maybe we can settle the score tonight and, I don't know, become friends?"

Friends. Thea didn't necessarily need more friends. Not that she had many to begin with. However, smoothing things over with Derek was a necessity. Neither of them were going anywhere. That was clear. That very afternoon after giving the final walkthrough to their clients, Tim had complimented both her and Derek's work on the project. She had to give it to him. He had everything done with time to spare.

"I'm just thinking about this morning when we both said we were going on dates and—"

"We had no idea it was with each other?" Thea filled in the gap.

"Yes! Yes, this is bizarre."

"Ridiculous."

"Right."

They settled into silence again.

It was awkward, but it didn't feel wrong.

"Maybe we should order something, and then we can ..." Thea began.

"Totally, good idea." Derek focused on his menu on the table.

Though Thea stared at all the options, she couldn't make sense of the words. The fact that Derek Harper was her blind date was still a staggering revelation. Even more than that, she was starting to like his company. He was right across the table from her, looking so handsome. Cleaner cut than she'd ever seen him on a work site. And his long hair that she'd always rolled her eyes at suddenly looked so tempting.

Thea shifted in her seat, recrossing her legs, and accidentally bumped her foot up against his leg. She withdrew from him as if he were a hot stove. "Sorry, sorry," she muttered softly.

"It's okay."

And his voice, *oh God*, his voice. Not deep, but resolute. Strong. Yet gentle.

What the hell is happening to me?

"Okay, I think I know what I want," Derek said.

"Me, too," Thea lied.

Their eyes met yet again. Then quickly darted away from each other like fish scared by someone tapping on the glass.

"Um ... so. Guitar," Thea said.

"Oh," he laughed nervously. "Yeah."

"How long have you been taking lessons?"

He shrugged. "With Zoe? Since she started taking students."

"Wow."

"Yeah, but I've played for a long time now."

"I had no idea."

"I like to keep it that way."

Thea cocked her head to the side. "Why is that?"

Derek opened his mouth to speak, then sealed his lips together, giving Thea a long moment to think about what power those lips might have over her. *This is happening so fast. He might hate my guts. Why am I feeling things?* "I'm not very good."

Her eyebrows rose up as she laughed.

"I'm serious."

"Oh, come on. That's ridiculous."

"You haven't heard me play; you have no idea."

"But to not even tell people that you play."

Derek shook his head, a wave of black hair falling over one eye. "I don't want to be one of those guys who says they can play guitar and then is shitty at guitar."

"Okay, well ..." Thea picked up her glass of wine and gestured it softly toward him. "From all the straight women out there, that is greatly appreciated."

He grinned. That beaming white smile. Beautiful and charming. "Well, you're all very welcome."

Thea eyed his tie. "You look really nice."

"Oh, thanks."

"Yeah, your date would have loved it."

Derek chuckled. "Yeah, yours would have too."

A third time, their eyes met. This time, they did not skitter away. Thea's heart fluttered. Regardless of what they called it afterward, they were on a date.

And Thea was suddenly very determined to enjoy Derek's company.

Chapter Four

He knew he was doomed from the moment she pulled the menu away from her face. Because the feeling Derek had upon seeing her was not one of dread. It was a thrill.

There would have been no world where Derek and Thea would have agreed to go out to dinner on their own, even only as colleagues. So the fact that they had been forced into his situation by chance gave Derek heart palpitations.

Well, that and the fact that Thea looked incredible. Her green leather dress tightly hugged her chest and exposed her collarbone. When she had gotten up to use the bathroom, he couldn't help but admire the way her curves looked as she walked away.

It was a risk to suggest they stay and have dinner anyway. Derek knew this.

But it was clearly paying off. Because, if he wasn't mistaken, they were having fun. Thea's face was flushed and red, and not with anger as it usually was when he was near. And she was nonstop giggles. Derek, to match, was alive with stories and eager to make her smile.

There was a gleam in her eye he wanted to ask her about. What was she thinking behind those hazy eyes? Every time he about got the nerve to ask, he backed away.

"Why did you get so interested in plants?" he asked instead.

"Oh, well, they're everywhere. They're hard to ignore."

Derek laughed as he lifted his wine glass. "That's true."

Thea scratched her head thoughtfully. "I don't know. There's always been something about them I've liked. They touch every sense. Sight, scent, touch, taste ..."

"You don't want to taste all of them, though."

"No, but that's part of it, isn't it? The variety of what plants offer us. They all work within the network of nature to provide something for some living thing. Whether or not it's us doesn't matter, does it?"

Derek felt a sense of intrigue with Thea when she said that. It wasn't often he met people who understood that the world wasn't made for humans and humans alone. There were checks and balances that humankind had been ignoring now for centuries. Slowly, their selfishness was causing the world to crumble.

However, all good things must come to an end. And this non-date had to draw to a close at some point. Neither of them had really wanted to be there in the first place. Even so, Derek would have stayed through the whole night.

Dinner was eaten, and the bottle of wine was nearly finished.

There was nothing left to do but pay the check and say goodnight.

And the thought of that caused an unexpected depression to fall over Derek.

"Any weekend plans?" he asked casually after clearing his throat.

"No. You're right about me. I mostly work," Thea said, then took the final sip of her wine.

"I was being an asshole, you know."

"Oh, I know you were. Doesn't mean you were wrong," Thea replied.

Derek laughed. Shocked by her sense of humor. Thea Winton knew how to make fun of herself and not take life so seriously. Who would have thought?

They were interrupted by their server dropping off the bill.

Without batting an eye, Derek pulled his wallet out of his pocket. Thea grabbed her clutch and started to do the same, but he shook his head. "I got it."

"No, we're splitting it."

"No, no. I'm getting it."

"Derek, don't be ridiculous, I picked out the expensive wine and—"

Derek reached across the table and grabbed Thea's hand. "Thea, I'm serious. I got it."

Thea widened her eyes.

Shit, I've gone too far. He removed his hand from hers and put his card down. He cleared his throat, scanning the restaurant for their server, hoping that by catching his eye he could end the awkward moment. "Um. Well, are you okay to drive?"

She chewed on her lower lip. "I'll finish my water. Then I'll be okay."

"I can take you home. I'm fine," he said, trying to veil his eagerness.

"I'm not going to make you do that. Besides, my car would be here and—"

"Well, I could bring you back in the morning."

Again, wide eyes.

"Not—I mean—I'd pick you up. From your house."

Thea shook her head. "Right, totally."

"And then bring you here."

"Yes, I understand."

Derek's heart was throbbing in his chest. Every time he crossed a line, her eyes got big. He couldn't tell if he was scaring her or if she was trying to read him.

"I thought for a second you were saying ..." Thea laughed to herself. "I'd sleepover or something."

"No, no way." *Dude, you are fucking this up.* "I mean ... that's not what I meant."

They locked their gazes. This was another thing that kept happening. Intense, steamy eye contact. Or it felt steamy to Derek.

"I'll take this, thanks," the server interrupted, grabbing the check.

Your timing sucks, my man.

Thea and Derek walked out into the quiet night, the summer sky big and dark over them with prickles of starlight.

He sighed contentedly. "Beautiful night."

"Yeah, it is."

They stood side by side looking up at the sky. Derek's gaze was slowly pulled back to Thea. She was beautiful. Much too beautiful for him, he decided. And if she'd made anything clear over the past nearly year of working together, she needed a man who could keep up with her and all her needs.

Derek wasn't sure he could keep up with even his own.

"I think you should take me home," Thea said suddenly. "My head is a little off."

"You all right?"

"Yeah, just shouldn't drive," Thea said softly.

"My truck's over here," he said, his voice weakening. Each step he took leading her to the truck, his blood pumped harder. He opened the passenger door for her. "It's kind of a big step."

Thea smiled. "That's okay. I'm a big girl."

Derek laughed but couldn't find a response. All he could focus on was her radiance. How the night made her hair look like sprays of purple heliotropes. Derek held out his hand for her and patted the inside of the cab. "Grab my right hand to pull yourself up if needed."

She took him up on his offer and gripped his hand as she reached for the door with the other to give herself a boost. A simple, helpful hand touch. That's what he tried to tell himself. He didn't have to make it more than that in his mind. But if it was nothing more than a friendly touch, why were his insides knotting together with want for her?

Thea tilted her head to the side. "Derek?"

"Yes?"

Her hand curled around his. "Thank you for dinner tonight."

"You're welcome.

"Thank you for staying."

Derek's gaze fell to Thea's lips. Fuck all the moments of consternation and frustration between them. The first impulse he'd had of her was that she was beautiful. And now, he wanted her. But bridging that gap felt impossible. "Of course, Thea."

She nodded before looking away. She stepped onto the truck step, hauling herself up to the cab.

Derek couldn't help himself. The tightening of his insides was too much to bear. He tugged on her hand and caught her in his arms, hugging her tight.

Thea gasped in surprise but made no effort to slip out of his grasp.

"There's something happening here," he whispered.

"I know," she said just as quietly.

He lowered his gaze to her lips and dared to lean closer. She leaned closer too. And then their lips met.

Her body melted into him. Chest to chest, pelvis to pelvis. Her warmth was everything he had craved the entire night.

Thea wrapped her arms around his neck, holding tightly to him. Her toes were barely grazing the ground. The tiniest moan escaped her. She broke the kiss but did not leave his airspace. Her lips grazed his chin.

"Would you like to go home with me?" he whispered.

She hummed happily. "Yes. Please."

The ride to Derek's bungalow was silent. What would happen next went unsaid. His body was buzzing, and he suspected hers was too. Restraining himself was difficult. He nearly ran three stop signs while his mind raced with thoughts of what was to come.

It was hard to believe how he was driving at top speed to get Thea into his home so he could make love to her. Not only because their relationship had always been strained, but because he hadn't dated in a long time.

For the first time in three years, a woman had made him feel something. And it was freakin' Thea Winton. Who would have guessed?

Derek thought he had been broken before. It turned out all he needed was to break through the tough act of his coworker.

Once parked in his driveway, Derek led Thea up to the house. They both stayed a respectful distance away from one another. Any slight touch would set them off in a direction they couldn't return from. Best get inside first.

"Um, this is my place," he muttered, opening the door for her.

Thea stepped through. "Thank you. It's lovely."

"It's dark, you can't even see it," Derek said wryly as he followed her inside. He flipped on a light so she could actually see the place. Though he didn't have the highest quality furniture, what he had was decent enough. His house was clean, thank goodness. The only sign of a mess was the basket of folded laundry sitting next to the stairs, waiting to be taken to his bedroom and put away.

"I'm trying to make polite conversation, is that so bad?" she asked with a cheeky smile. She kicked off her shoes before going over to the staircase. Grabbing the newel post, she leaned to the side to look into the darkness of the second floor. "Your room is upstairs?"

Derek raised his brows.

"Don't look surprised," she admonished him with a laugh.

"I'm just … You're so forward!"

"Would you like me to slow down?"

"No, I …" Derek walked over to her and stopped a step away. Close enough to take her, far enough away to keep the anticipation building. "Didn't expect this from you."

Her lips curled to the side. "Well, Derek, I'm full of surprises. Just like you. And your guitar playing."

"That's a little different then…" Derek trailed off as Thea began to ascend the stairs.

"Don't keep me waiting too long, Derek," she said in a tone so sensual it made his heart ache. Then she disappeared onto the second floor, leaving nothing but the smell of her shampoo.

Derek stared after her, eyes wide as moons. This was really happening. He could barely believe it.

With a *fuck it* to any last bit of restraint, Derek scrambled up the stairs and found Thea waiting for him in his bedroom. "Help me with my zipper, will you?"

Derek approached her from behind and carefully touched the zipper on the back of her dress. Delicately, he pulled it down her back inch by inch, revealing her silken skin. He leaned his head down and pressed a kiss to the apex of her back. He trailed the kisses up the back of her neck and into her sprays of curls. Carefully, he placed his hands on her shoulder blades and inched the sleeves of her dress off her shoulders.

Thea let the dress fall down the rest of her body, leaving her almost completely exposed except for a tiny pair of panties that covered barely anything.

He swallowed. "Oh, God."

"Is that a good or a bad 'oh, God?'"

"Good. Very good, Thea. You're stunning."

Thea took his hands in hers and placed them against her hips, guiding them up the length of her body to her breasts. The way they filled his hands was magical. "You haven't even seen me from the front."

"I might pass out if I do."

Turning quickly, Thea caught him in a kiss. Derek stumbled a step backward; Thea was in control. She grabbed his tie and pulled him with her until they tumbled back onto the bed, her naked body beneath him. "I can feel you," she whispered between kisses. Her hand slid to his crotch and cupped him earnestly.

"Oh, shit."

"Am I hurting you?"

"No! I just ..." *Want to be good for you. Want to last for you.* No words came out.

Thea delicately undid the closure on his pants.

Derek pushed himself up from the bed and shook off his pants and suit jacket. Then, he began to work on the green tie. "I want to feel all of you. You know?" His gaze fell on Thea's body. Luscious curves, perky nipples, the line of her neck as she gazed up at him from the bed.

Thea nodded and invited him back between her legs. "I know."

She helped him with his shirt, unbuttoning from the bottom, while he started from the top. When their fingers met, they both laughed shyly. Thea ran her hands up his bare chest. "Goddamn, Derek. Hiding all this under your tank tops."

"Well, always keep 'em wanting more."

"You could say that," Thea whispered.

Wordlessly she lifted her hips for him. Derek hooked his fingers around her panties and pulled them down.

Thea reached up for him, pulling him toward her lips. "Come here."

Derek moaned into her mouth and broke away. "No."

Before Thea could protest, Derek opened a drawer in the nightstand and pulled out a condom. Moments later, with the protection in place, he wrapped his hands around her hips and hauled her up onto his lap. She gasped, straddling his knees and causing their most intimate parts to press together.

"This is about you. I want you to feel good."

Thea cupped his cheeks in her hands, smiling. "I already feel good."

He pressed a line of kisses up her jaw until he reached her ear. "I want to make you feel incredible." Derek started rocking his hips under her, rubbing their bodies together. "You do what feels right. I'm yours tonight, Thea."

She lifted her hips, positioned him at her entrance, and then lowered herself onto him, breath tightening as he stretched her. "Oh, Derek, you feel ..."

His head was buzzing with his own arousal. He had not been welcomed inside somebody for years. He had not wanted this so badly in years.

Thea began to rub her hips against him, taking him deeper. "You feel so good."

He rested his hands on the small of her back.

With a trembling moan, Thea's head fell back, curls bouncing as she rode him.

"On top of me," Thea whimpered several minutes later. "Need you on top of me."

Something in Derek snapped. In a fluid motion, he flipped Thea onto her back and began to pound into her faster and faster. Thea's legs locked around his hips, her moans vibrating against his neck. Finally, Thea's body seized beneath him, a roar spilling from her mouth. She was coming. He could feel her tense around him, pleading with him to come too.

And Derek's body was eager to oblige. He bucked his hips hard, grunting as his body was overcome with the shock of pleasure. Stars danced in his vision as his head drooped like a wilting flower.

Thea raked her hands through his hair, clutching his head softly between her palms. She guided him down to her chest and held him there tight.

Derek could feel her heart beating in his cheek. Their bodies were sweaty and blisteringly hot.

But he couldn't bear to tear himself away from her.

"You feel amazing," Thea whispered against the crown of his head.

Derek slipped his arms under her, hugging her tightly.

Tonight, he would not let her go.

He'd hold her even longer if she'd let him.

Chapter Five

When Thea blinked awake the next morning and saw Derek lying beside her, she immediately felt like she'd made a huge mistake.

It wasn't that she didn't enjoy herself. In fact, the night had been exquisite. Derek was an incredible lover. He was giving and enthusiastic, caring much more about her pleasure than his.

Waking up to him just reminded her she could never have that again.

It was all a comedy of errors. An accidental setup, a wine-flushed kiss, tripping into bed together.

A fluke. That's what it was. A glorious, one-time fluke.

Because in no world was Thea going to be risking her job in order to gallivant around with Derek Harper. Regardless of how good the sex was.

"Good morning," Derek grumbled, head still turned into the pillow.

Thea stared at him.

He shimmied closer, putting his hand into the bend of her waist. His thumb traveled across her skin softly. "How'd you sleep?"

She wanted him again. A single touch. That's all it took. "We can't do this again," she blurted.

Derek lifted his head, eyes heavy with sleep. His bedhead was somehow even sexier than his hair from the previous night. "Huh?"

Thea delicately removed his hand from her waist. "I don't do things like this often."

"Oh, yeah. Me neither."

Yeah, right. "And, you know, we work together."

"Right."

"So, we shouldn't do this again."

Derek cleared his throat and shook his head to rid himself of the hangover of sleep. "I'm sorry, did you have a bad time?" he asked, an innocent smallness to his voice. "Should I not have—"

"No! Oh my god, no. I don't want you to—" *Shit.* "I had an amazing time."

The corner of his mouth turned upward.

"And we can't do it again because that could make things messy."

Derek frowned but nodded slowly. "A-all right."

"This isn't because I don't like you. I do like you. I think. I mean you're a pain in the ass at work, but—"

He laughed meekly. "I get what you mean." Then his brown eyes flicked up to Thea's. Took her breath away. Warm and inviting. So much more depth than she'd ever noticed before. "I had fun. And we don't have to do it again."

"Great."

"Great."

It did not feel great.

It was quickly decided that they would get ready to go, and Derek would take Thea to get her car. Nearly as quickly, they were dressed and walking out to Derek's pickup truck. Unlike the night before, he did not open her door or hold out his hand for her. There would be no possibility of her tumbling into his arms again for a languid kiss.

Things were going back to the way they had always been. Business.

The ride would have been completely silent if Derek hadn't turned on the radio. "Do you have a preference for what to listen to?"

"Whatever you like."

Derek turned on the top forty, which Thea *knew* wasn't what he listened to. He was trying to be accommodating. To be a good guy.

It made her like him more.

When he pulled into the restaurant parking lot, he nodded. "All right. Well. Get home safe."

"Yeah. You too." Thea put her hand on her door. *Stop me. Do something.* "Thanks again." She opened it.

"No problem. Happy to do it."

Thea glanced back at Derek once more. If there was a world where she had stayed in bed with Derek and allowed his arms to wind around her as they whispered to each other various sweet nothings, Thea would not allow herself to see it.

She had to go.

"You look like hell," Zoe mumbled as soon as Thea stepped into the house.

"Gee, thanks."

The second Derek had dropped her off, Thea drove to Zoe's house. Or should she say Marty's house? She still wasn't sure, even though Zoe had been living there for four months. It felt weird to think that nearly every time she visited her friend at home, there was a six-year-old around watching cartoons.

"Ella, can you say hi to Thea?" Zoe called out.

Ella poked her head over the couch and waved. "Hi, Thea."

"Hi, Ella." Thea wasn't a whiz with kids, not like Zoe was. Ella, though, was one of those special kids who was good at alleviating adults' uneasiness. So Thea was usually pleased to see her.

"Are you here to play?" the little girl asked.

Thea gulped. "Um ..."

"Thea and I are going to talk. Maybe she'll play later."

Ella's face fell. "Mmph. Okay." Then she slid back onto the couch to watch the television.

Thea eyed Zoe. "The kid needs a sibling."

Zoe went beet red. "Aren't you the one that always says we're moving too fast? Let me get a year in before you start thinking about my ovaries."

The subject change didn't distract Thea for long. "Is Marty home?"

"He won't judge you for your walk of shame," Zoe murmured.

Thea huffed. "We need to talk. Privately."

"Yeesh, okay. We'll go in the dining room."

Zoe led Thea into the dining room and sat at the table. "So, I'm assuming it went well?"

Thea was not in a sitting mood. "It did not go well. Not at all."

Her friend lifted her brows. "Then care to enlighten me on the outfit?"

Thea gripped her hands in fists. "You set me up with Derek Harper."

"Yeah. He's cute, right?"

"No, he's not cute. He's my *coworker*," Thea squeezed through her teeth.

Zoe was not nearly as stressed about the situation, holding back a peel of laughter. "Oh, *shit*."

"You set me up for the most mortifying experience of my life and all you have to say is oh ..." Thea glanced over her shoulder to make sure Ella was tuned into the television and wouldn't hear her curse.

"How was I supposed to know?"

"You teach him guitar lessons! Surely you talk about other things besides that."

Zoe shrugged. "I mean, we do, but I haven't really talked to him about work."

Pressing her hands to her eyes, Thea whined, "This is awful."

"Thea, it couldn't have been that bad. You're wearing the clothes you wore last night, surely that means—"

"Yes, we slept together! What do you want from me?"

"Morning, Thea."

Thea turned around with wild eyes to find Marty in the entryway of the dining room. "Oh. Great. Now Marty knows."

"Marty doesn't care," Zoe reiterated.

He looked between the women as he worked on buttoning the last button on his loudly patterned shirt. "I'll just go watch some *Bluey* in the other room."

"Good idea, babe," Zoe said with a smile.

Marty gave Thea a quick look and practically scurried away like a mouse being sized up by a cat.

"Okay. You slept with your coworker. I get it. Complicated."

"More than complicated. Embarrassing."

"Why? Was it bad?"

"No, but that's not the point, Zo."

Zoe waved her hands. "I don't think there's a problem here. "

"There is a problem. We don't like each other at work. He's probably going to tell all the guys at work that he got in my pants and saw me naked and that I'm bad in the sack or—"

"Was it bad or not, Thea?"

Thea pursed her lips and shook her head. "No, it was really good."

Zoe smiled smugly.

"Don't smile at me like that."

"I'm not smiling any type of way."

The two women were silent. From the other room, the sounds of *Bluey* could be heard playing as Marty and Ella were engaged in a conversation about shoe tying.

"So, wait. He showed up. You both were like, 'Oh, hey it's you' and then ..."

Thea sunk into a chair. "Then we had dinner because, why not if we went all that way? And then he paid and then—"

"So he treated it like a date."

"Yeah, I guess."

"I knew he'd be a gentleman," Zoe said, still smiling.

Thea collapsed over the table and groaned. "You're not helping."

"What would be so bad about maybe going out again?"

"We're not allowed to. They can fire us at will. And dating in the company isn't allowed."

"Mm. That's stupid."

Thea would have fought her on that yesterday. Workplace relationships usually got in the way. She had disdain for fraternizing. However, now that she was caught in its grips, she was inclined to agree.

"Why not just, like, do a little secret thing? You know."

Thea lifted her head. "What?"

"Like friends with benefits or lovers?" Zoe grinned excitedly.

"Zoe, I hate to tell you this, but this is my life. Not a romcom. So—"

"Right, it's your life. You get to decide what you want to do."

Thea blinked, her dark lashes clumped with yesterday's mascara.

"You had fun. You had good sex. He paid for dinner. These are all good things."

"That could put my job in jeopardy, Zoe."

"They can't fire you for flirting! You could at least do that."

Maybe. "I can't afford to make any mistakes. Literally and"—Thea paused and took a breath—"I want this to work."

"I know you do."

"I can't risk losing my job because of some good sex."

"Is that all it was?" Zoe asked earnestly.

Thea wouldn't allow it to be anything more. She was good about that. Compartmentalizing. And because she had decided that this was a one-night thing, it would be just that. However, if she was more honest with herself, there was a pull deep in her gut telling her that she wanted more Derek Harper.

"Just think about it. You deserve to have fun. And I know that you can make something like that work. All it requires are late nights in the privacy of your homes. No eyes on you, no problem."

"It's just not possible."

Zoe hesitated. "All right."

"Hey, I'm headed to the restaurant," Marty announced, popping his head back into the dining room.

Zoe leaped to her feet and went to her boyfriend, pecking him on the lips.

"Good to see you, Thea," Marty said.

"Yeah, you too ..." Thea sighed without looking back at the man. Her mind was too clogged with thoughts of Derek Harper and a future she could never have.

She wasn't that type of girl.

Chapter Six

Derek was rarely on time and certainly never early.

But Monday was different. He wanted to turn a new leaf. That's what he told himself, at least, to avoid the fact that what he really wanted was to make a good impression on Thea.

Since Saturday morning, when she had told him that what they had done was ... well, a mistake, he'd been nursing a crack in his heart. It was hard to believe after months of constantly butting heads that he'd be lamenting her absence in his life and yet, here he was. Thinking in circles about ways to get Thea Winton back in his life.

However, he knew Thea was stubborn. When she set her mind to something, that's what she would do. And if she had set her mind to pretending like the night they shared never happened, Derek would have to accept that's how it was going to be.

That didn't mean he couldn't at least nurture a friendship with her, right? Maybe they could make work more pleasant.

Today was a perfect day to do so. They were starting a new job funded by a public works grant: developing the back half of Centennial Park in downtown Cloverton. It had fallen into disrepair: a lopsided wooden barn that should have been torn down, broken benches, and brittle pavement. It was in need of a total refresh.

And Tate Landscaping and Construction was just the company to do it, not to mention, the only one in the area.

When Derek arrived at a quarter to nine, the site was already bustling with activity. He strapped on his tool belt and waded through the pallets of sod and wood to where all his coworkers were congregating.

"*Sup*, D?" his buddy, Hamilton, called out. "How was the date?"

Derek blanched. "Good."

Hamilton laughed. "Good? You look like you might soil yourself."

He swallowed. "I don't really want to talk about it."

Hamilton smiled sympathetically and patted Derek on the shoulder. "You'll find someone eventually, D." Hamilton had been a good friend since Derek started working at Tate. He was around the same age and in that same place in life where he felt a little too young to settle down and a little too old to not be thinking about it. The difference was that Hamilton had charm and charisma; ladies seemed to flock to him.

"Everyone gather round," Tim Tate, their boss, called out.

The workers all started congregating around the middle of the park. Derek's eyes darted around, trying to catch a glimpse of Thea ... wherever she was.

"Big day today, folks. Big job. Important job." Tim Tate was not a Cloverton native. He'd moved into town a little less than a year prior to managing the Cloverton branch of Tate Landscaping. His speeches before new jobs always felt a little hollow, as he didn't *really* understand the town and its dynamics. Even though Derek wasn't a native, he at least had taken the time to figure out what Cloverton was all about. Place, to Derek, was important. Just as important as his loved ones.

"This is a three-month job that we're doing in one. So everyone needs to be on their A-game, all right? I'll be around more often than usual, but Thea is going to be in charge of the day-to-day logistics. Thea, are you around?"

"Here!"

Derek snapped his attention in the direction of her voice. Thea was sneaking through the crowd of workers, holding various rolls of documents. Her curly hair was pinned back out of her face and her makeup was crisp and neat.

Derek couldn't stand how perfect she looked in his eyes.

"There she is," Tim said with a smile.

"Sorry, I was gathering some last minute—"

"Thea is in charge, so don't give her a hard time, all right, boys?"

Derek glanced at Rita, the only woman on the team who worked regularly. She had stopped trying to correct Tim's language to be more inclusive and instead started flipping him off out of his eyeline.

"Thanks, Tim. I have come up with teams for the projects. Most importantly, this first week is the cleanup effort. We need to get everything in tip-top shape before we start on our bigger projects," Thea explained and then started rattling off the groupings of who was working where. There was the bandshell team, working on erecting a barn-like structure to host concerts and events, then the overhaul of the walkways, and, of course, the natural elements. Flowers, sod, hedges. "On the visuals, I have Derek, Hamilton, and Rita. I'd like to talk to you three in the office so we can go over the vision and the technical aspects."

Derek gulped.

"Other than that, that's it. Your point person already has the plans. Let's get started," Thea explained.

"Thanks, Thea," Tim said with a dismissive smile. "You heard the woman. Get going."

Thea's eyes immediately found Derek's, cutting directly into his soul. He'd known it would be weird to see her, he just didn't anticipate it would be difficult. The wanting was still so strong inside him. To go back to how things used to be would break his heart.

Thea cleared her throat. "Fountain team, follow me."

Derek, Hamilton, and Rita followed Thea to the office, which was a trailer in the parking lot of the park, with fans blasting in every window to make it actually hospitable to life forms.

Derek did his best not to watch her hips sway from side to side in her tight-fitting khaki shorts, but it was damn near impossible. It would be impossible to forget Thea's body now that he knew it.

Especially if she was going to be floating around the work site all day.

Things were cramped in the trailer. The three workers stood at one end of the card table in the middle of the space while Thea unrolled her plan. "Ideally, we're going to make the garden as self-sustaining as possible." She pointed to the images on the paper. "Prairie flowers and grasses. Things that don't need significant upkeep and can also serve as education about the botany of the area."

Derek peered down at the lists of flowers and how she had laid them out in the plots.

"The only stipulation made by city hall was that there had to be a significant presence of *Viola sororia*," Thea explained.

"*Viola sororia* can choke out other plants," Derek interjected and immediately regretted it when he saw the surprise on Thea's face. A week ago, he would have happily interrupted her and been gleeful at her annoyance.

Now he felt like it was adding insult to injury.

To his surprise though, Thea smirked. "I know that, Derek."

"Yeah, she knows that, Derek," Hamilton reiterated in a teasing fashion.

"Just making sure that it's ... you know, known."

Thea nodded. "It's known."

Derek's heart sped up in his chest. For once, she wasn't getting huffy. She was playing along.

"It's the state flower of Illinois. I don't think we're getting out of it being a part of the garden," Thea said. "Any suggestions?"

Suggestions? Thea had never asked the landscapers for suggestions. She always came in knowing plan a, b, *and* c.

"We keep them separate. As best we can. Use ground ivy as a buffer, maybe," Rita posited.

"We don't really have enough real estate for that," Thea said.

Hamilton shrugged. "Pot 'em."

"We're not potting them, dumbass. It's a native garden," Rita said to Hamilton.

"I'm just saying. Violets can be nasty."

An idea sprung to Derek's head; he opened his mouth and then quickly closed it.

"What?" Thea asked, noticing that he was holding back.

Derek bit his lower lip. "Nothing. Nope."

"Derek, I saw you open your mouth," she said with a bobble of her head.

His mind went straight into the gutter. All the things they'd done with open mouths the other night. Kissing, sucking, devouring. "You're not going to like it."

Thea crossed her arms and leaned into her hip. "Try me."

"Thea."

"*Derek*."

Hamilton frowned in confusion. "Hamilton."

Rita punched him in the side.

"Well, most people can't tell the difference between violet varietals, right?" Derek asked. "But if we pick a different varietal, perhaps *Viola riviniana*, then we're pulling back on the issue of invasiveness and spread. Can use a buffer of ground ivy or clover that's a bit weaker and—"

Thea nodded. "I see what you're getting at."

"*Riviniana*, what's that?" Rita frowned.

"Dog violet," Thea answered.

Derek held back a small smile. He knew that Thea had a handle on all the technical bits, but hearing her work was making him swoon.

"It'd be a bit dishonest. Don't you think?" Thea asked, narrowing her eyes.

"You want violets?" Derek shrugged.

"I want violets."

"Well, then, best of both worlds."

She frowned. "It's not that simple, you know."

"There was a reason I didn't want to tell you my suggestion," he said, leaning up against the wall of the trailer.

"Yeah, makes sense now."

The trailer fell quiet.

"Well, keep thinking about it. Today start carving out the plots and working on the sod."

"Got it, boss," Hamilton said with a nod.

Derek's team left without him. He still had a bone to pick with Thea. But she wasn't paying attention to him, rolling her plan back up and clearing off the table.

"Why'd you have to do that?"

"Do what?"

"Embarrass me like that."

Thea looked up. "I wasn't trying to embarrass you."

"Well, you made me tell you my idea. Which is a pretty good idea, if you ask me."

She smiled awkwardly. "Yeah, if we want to lie."

"If you're looking to make a garden without any up-keep—"

"I didn't say *any*."

"Whatever." Derek threw his hands up.

Thea gaped at him. "Don't 'whatever' me. It would never work! Dog violet doesn't even have a scent!"

"It's a garden, there will be *plenty* of scents."

She let out a sound of frustration and waved him off. "I thought we might be able to get along on this, but maybe I was wrong."

"Don't sell me short like that."

"I'm not! I thought that maybe we'd be able to put our differences aside and ..." Thea trailed off as her eyes met Derek's. Then, she shook it off. "Never mind. Let's just get out there, huh?"

Thea stepped past him toward the exit, but Derek couldn't control himself. He put his arm up in front of her and leaned over her. "Are we really going to pretend like nothing happened?"

Her eyes widened. "Derek."

"I get it, you know. I understand that nothing more can happen, but are we really going to be jerks to each other about it?"

"I'm not trying to be a jerk."

"Well, then maybe you can act like you like me for a second instead of acting like I'm some pesky fly in your ear."

Thea gasped. "That's not how I'm acting!"

"That's how it feels!"

Derek suddenly realized how close they had gotten. Their faces were only a couple of inches apart. Both were breathing heavily like they had after they had given one another the deepest kind of pleasure.

"Derek," Thea said, her voice small. "I'm trying really hard to make sure we can still work together." She touched his arm and guided it down from the wall back to his side.

"I don't want to just work together," Derek said without thinking. "I mean— What I mean is—" He took a deep breath. "Can we be nice? You don't have to like what I say, but ..."

"I'll be nicer. I will. I'm sorry," Thea replied. "It's a good idea. I just have to think about it. You know that's not how I usually operate."

He knew she was talking about the violets but secretly wished she was talking about him. That *they* would be a good idea, in some respect. "Okay. That's ... yeah."

She smiled meekly, and then walked out of the trailer, leaving him in her wake.

Derek took a moment to recenter himself. *You'll get over her. It takes time.* Yet the entire day, he watched her from the corner of his eye, trying to pretend his body and soul weren't yearning for her.

When he got home that night, he went right for his guitar to unwind from the day. None of his usual songs released his tension. He muted the strings and took a deep breath. *Don't do it. Don't.*

But he had to.

Strumming a chord, he sang out softly, "Hazy blue. Too easy to get lost in you ..."

Over the course of the next hour, hopping from rhyme to rhyme and chord to chord, Derek stumbled into a song. Just for Thea.

Chapter Seven

A week prior, Thea had been sitting at dinner with Derek, losing herself in his warm brown eyes and the luscious bottle of wine.

Now, she was standing at her kitchen counter eating a microwaved tamale and wondering what the hell was wrong with her.

They had made it through the week with only a couple of close calls. There was the argument in the trailer on Monday when she was too harsh with him because, inside, she was panicking over her attraction to him. Then on Wednesday, she was helping the visuals team with weeding and got stuck next to Derek for a whole hour while they dug stinging nettles out of the ground as carefully as possible so he could take them home and sauté them, which she found absolutely insane. And then there was the way he said goodbye only a few hours ago.

The day had been horrendously hot. His white tank top was soaked through, so much so that she could see the outlines of his six-pack and tight pecs. It bothered her. In a good way. And as they both walked to their cars at the end of the day, he'd made a point to call out to her from his truck, that smooth smile on his lips. "Thea, have a good weekend."

"You too," she barely managed to squeak.

It was a harmless nicety, right? Maybe. But Thea couldn't help but feel it was more. *Have a good weekend, and try not to remember what happened during the last one!*

She remembered all right. Every fucking detail. Didn't matter that her mind was clouded with wine. That night with Derek was the most visceral and earth-shaking night of her life. How could she not remember?

It caught her off guard throughout the week. She'd be standing somewhere about to do something and then slip into the memory of Derek's hot breath on her neck. On more than one occasion, Tim had caught her and given her shit for it. "Look alive, Thea!" or "Where you off to, champ?"

Little did he know that she was locked into a memory about a steamy night with her coworker. If he could read her mind, she'd lose her job.

Now, though, alone, with every opportunity to reflect on the week, Thea was sad. Lonely. Zoe was with Ella, and all her other friends were linked up with their partners for the evening. Even her own mom and dad were taking a weekend away.

Loneliness, for Thea, was a more powerful drug than alcohol. It could make her do stupid things. Like texting an ex or making a huge impulse purchase she would immediately regret.

Friends with benefits.

Maybe Zoe was right. Maybe there were other options for her and Derek. Ones that would keep their attraction a secret. That wouldn't get them too deeply entangled. That could keep them safe.

Thea pulled out her phone and took a deep breath.

Tonight, she was going to do what would debatably be the stupidest thing she'd ever done in the name of loneliness.

She was going to call Derek.

Her anxiety buzzed as she pressed his contact and put the phone to her ear. The only times she had ever called him were when he was running late. And for those calls, he never picked up. It was more a symbolic thing than anything. To let him know that she was annoyed.

So she had no idea how he would sound picking up the phone. Or even *if* he would pick up the phone.

"Thea?"

Her body shivered at the sound of her name coming from his mouth.

"Everything okay?"

"Y-yeah, everything's okay. Just needed to talk to you about something."

"If it's about work, I'm off the clock," he replied, half-joking.

Thea cleared her throat. This was her last out. She could pretend she was calling about work and have a quick two-minute phone call before hanging up and going to her bed alone in shame.

Or she could follow through.

"I think you should come over."

Derek was silent.

"There's something I want to talk to you about."

Still, silence.

Thea's heartbeat so loudly in her chest that she thought he might be able to hear it.

"Okay. What's your address?"

A short half hour later, Thea was sitting at her kitchen table drinking a cup of dandelion tea. Derek had brought a jar of dried dandelion flowers as a hostess gift and brewed it himself.

Now, they were sitting across from each other. And Thea had just dropped a bomb.

"Friends with benefits?" Derek repeated, steam curling up into his face.

"Yeah, something like that."

He sipped his tea and frowned, his dark brow looking inky and luscious. "Huh."

"I know, it's kind of weird, but—"

"I thought nothing could happen between us. That's what you said on Saturday. And Monday."

Thea scratched her temple embarrassingly. "Yeah, I think I was saying that more for myself. Because I had a lot of fun last week with you."

Derek smiled softly.

Don't smile at me like that or I'll have to jump your bones here and now. "And I know that anything more would be dangerous between us. What with work and everything. So maybe if we just keep it really casual and friendly—"

"With some benefits, perhaps?" he teased.

"Yeah, exactly," Thea laughed.

They both went quiet and sipped their tea.

"I've just been thinking about you a lot."

Derek hummed. "I've been thinking about you a lot too."

Carefully, Thea raised her gaze to Derek's. She wanted to draw her eyes away but stayed captured by his deep brown eyes.

"Okay. Sure. We can try something," he said.

Thea smiled. "Really?"

"Yeah, we just have to be careful and set some ground rules, right?"

"Of course. Ground rules. I love ground rules."

"I know you do. You love rules of any kind."

Thea blushed. "You say that like it's a bad thing."

"For me, yes. For you, no. It's charming."

She took a deep breath. "Okay." Her voice wavered. Being alone with Derek in her house was as powerful an aphrodisiac as any. "Well, nothing at work."

"Easy."

"And keep it casual. You know. We can hang, we can ... have ... you know."

"Are you scared to say sex?" he asked with a cocky smile.

"N-no."

"Then say it."

Thea huffed in frustration. "Okay, new rule, stop being a pain in my ass."

"When you stop being a pain in mine."

They exchanged a charged look. Not angry. Heated. Something was already brewing tonight.

"Fine. Mutually stop being pains in asses," Thea acknowledged.

"And you say *sex*."

Thea tapped her foot on the ground in annoyance. "Fine. Sex."

"Wow. Incredible."

She laughed. "You're so rude."

"I'm just giving you a hard time. Just ..." Derek reached out and pushed a curl away from her forehead. "Just teasing you."

Thea sighed, eyes fluttering shut. She leaned her face toward his hand. "I like when you tease me."

"Yeah?"

"Yeah."

Derek pushed himself out of his seat and rounded the table to face her. "Thea?"

She stared up at him. "What?"

"I'm going to have you now. Is that all right?"

More than all right. It was necessary. "Yes."

Derek scooped her up into his arms without so much as batting an eye. Thea yelped but didn't for a second feel as though he might drop her. She looped her arms around his neck and planted a kiss on his lips.

The memory of his touch came flooding back to her. Already she could feel her center pulsing with need.

Derek carried her over to the kitchen counter and set her down. He bent down and began planting needy kisses on her neck, his hands sliding down the sides of her body. "You're a goddess."

She laughed. "No."

"I'm serious. You're perfect." He kissed her nose softly. "More than perfect."

Thea swooned.

"I wanna taste you," Derek whispered and then kissed her again. "May I taste you?"

"You're so polite."

Derek chuckled. "Is that bad?"

"No, it makes me want you."

He threw his head back in laughter, his mane of hair falling over his shoulders. "Why am I not surprised?" Derek slid his hands around her thighs and pushed her dress up to her hips, revealing her underwear. He dropped his head to her chest and began to pepper kisses from her collarbone to her sternum, slowly working the underwear off her legs with his hands.

Thea clutched the back of his head to her chest and moaned in relief. "I've needed you all week."

"Is that right?" he murmured before capturing the collar of her dress between his teeth and pulling it down to reveal her breasts.

"Mmm."

Derek captured one of her nipples between his lips.

Thea jerked, gasping with sudden arousal. "I'm glad you came over."

"Yeah, me too."

She tilted her head back and smiled. "You want to stay?"

"If you want me to."

Thea touched the fabric of his white T-shirt, pulling at it teasingly. "Oh, I definitely do. I'm not nearly tired. Got quite a few ideas for how we can pass the time."

"Do you, now?"

She bit her lip. "Yes. Except I'm going to be the one making you squirm."

Derek's eyebrows jumped. "O-okay. Not going to say no to that."

Thea leaped off the counter, took Derek by the hand, and tugged him out of the kitchen. "Come on, let me show you *my* bedroom."

Chapter Eight

Thea looked amazing. Well, she looked amazing every day. But today, she looked particularly amazing. She was wearing a fitted khaki romper that made her look like she was on a safari or some sort of expedition.

"No, this is wrong, the path needs to be at least a foot to the left." Her voice carried all the way from the bandshell construction. She was pointing to the beginnings of a gravel path that evidently was not to her specs.

He used to find it unbearable when she bossed people around. Now he loved it. She was direct and to the point, unflinching from what she wanted.

She was Thea.

For the past three weeks, Derek had liked work. Because where there was work, there was Thea. And any moment he wasn't working, he was thinking about her.

The two of them had settled into their friends-with-benefits arrangement. It felt inevitable, the way they folded together and giggled beneath the sheets.

At first, they were restrained. Some visits over the weekend and minor flirting after work.

But in the last week, things had heated up so significantly that Derek was having a hard time keeping his head on straight. Thea had spent every night at his house for five days straight. In the morning, they would go to work in their own cars, pretend like they were seeing each other for the first time that morning, and get to work. When they left, they'd both drive to Derek's and recommence their affair.

It wasn't only physical though. It had started to become mental as well. In those moments after winding their bodies together and making each other feel as if they could burst into a million stars, they connected. Deeply.

"What do you want?" Thea had asked him the night before, her breath hot in his ear.

"Hm?"

"With life. What do you want in life?"

"Big question."

She hummed in laughter. "I know. And I expect a big answer."

Derek had pulled her closer to his chest and sighed. "Where do I start?"

"Wherever you want."

It took Derek quite a while before he began speaking. "I want a big garden with lots of flowers."

"Of course."

"And someone to plant it with."

Their eyes met and even in the dark, he could see Thea blush.

"That's a nice thing to want."

"Yeah. And it would have one of those chairs that you could swing on. And a bird bath."

"Very idyllic."

"Hmm."

They lay there a little while longer, Derek tracing his fingers up and down Thea's arm, his heart galloping with nervousness.

"I want all that too," Thea whispered.

"Well, I hope we both find it."

"Yeah."

Thea fell asleep on his chest. And right there he decided that he wanted all of that with *her*. The two of them together would make a beautiful garden. Flourishing, full of bees and butterflies, and squirrels collecting nuts and, if he let his mind go there, he could see the garden as a metaphor for the family he wanted to create someday.

Thea's curly hair and his tan skin? They'd be beyond adorable.

Of course, in the morning, he squelched the thought way, way down to avoid crossing any lines. After all, friends with benefits didn't really allow for musing about a future garden together, let alone a future family.

Still, though, he couldn't ignore the feeling.

Derek was already looking forward to another night with Thea. What things would they discover about each other? How deep would she let him in? Both literally and metaphorically.

He wanted to touch her soul.

However, just because work and his affair were technically separate didn't mean that thoughts of Thea didn't spill over into his day-to-day life.

"Harper? Hello?"

"Huh? What?!" Derek nearly leaped out of his skin at the sound of his boss's voice. He turned to find Tim Tate on the edge of the garden, arms crossed over his chest, making his paunchy belly look even paunchier. "Tim! What's up?"

"Did you hear my question?"

Derek swallowed. "Sorry, could you repeat it?"

Tim sighed, rolling his eyes. "You were distracted again."

Again. Yes, this wasn't the first time Tim had shaken Derek back to reality. "Sorry, sir. It's so hot out here."

"Drink water, then. That's what I do." Tim carried around a gallon jug of water and guzzled it down throughout the day. He had to from how much he sweated.

"Thanks for the tip, sir."

"I asked you how the sprinklers are coming along. Can I expect them to be done by the end of the day?"

Today had been a grueling task for the visuals team. They were installing the in-ground sprinklers that were going to make the plots of flowers and native plant gardens as self-sustaining as possible. This involved digging small trenches to install PVC pipes all along the garden area to reach the valve box, then installing the pipes, and finally, at least for today, installing the sprinklers.

Derek surveyed the scene. "We're at a good pace."

"That's not what I asked. Can I expect them to be done by the end of the day?"

Derek glanced over at Hamilton and Rita who were bickering over the placement of one of the PVC pipes. "I think so."

"Think? I can't run my business on *think*, Derek."

"*Yes*. It will be done by the end of the day."

Tim's grim demeanor shifted, and he smiled. "Great!" Then, he wandered off in search of other employees to give a hard time to.

I'll show you great, Derek thought. If there was one thing that made Derek thrive, it was a grudge.

"Okay, nearly there," Derek grunted, wiping off his forehead with his T-shirt.

The visuals team was in the midst of the final step with the sprinkler install when the clock hit five.

"Damn. We were so close," Hamilton groaned.

"Oh, well. Pick it up tomorrow," Rita replied.

"You guys go. I'm going to finish this up," Derek said, getting to his feet and stretching.

Hamilton looked at his friend like he was crazy. "You sure, D?"

Derek nodded. "Yeah. I promised Tim we'd be done. And I don't want him giving us a hard time tomorrow."

Rita and Hamilton exchanged a look.

"You guys don't have to stay. Don't feel bad," Derek assured them. "Promise."

And with that assurance, Rita and Hamilton hopped to it, waving goodbye as they left the job site.

In all his years of working, Derek had never liked working late. He avoided it at any cost.

Now, though, things were different.

Thea was rubbing off on him. He'd made a promise to Tim, a stupid promise. In the past, he would have asked for forgiveness, not permission. Now, though, he was more interested in staying in his employer's good graces.

Which meant staying late.

And staying late meant the delayed gratification of getting Thea back in his arms.

However, he knew that she'd respect him for staying. And he wanted Thea's respect in any way, shape, or form he could get it.

Because deep inside him, he wanted her. More than her body. Friends with benefits was fine for now.

Someday, though, he hoped it would change.

"Hey, did you hear the final bell?" Thea called out to him.

Derek turned to look at her with a sigh. "Yeah, but I'm staying late. Want this done."

Thea examined the trenches of PVC pipe and the few sprinklers still waiting to be installed. "You can get it done tomorrow."

"Well, you were hoping to have it done today," he said. "And I promised Tim it would be done. So it'll be better for everyone if I get it done."

"I can deal with Tim."

Derek nodded. "I know you can. I just don't want it on your plate."

Thea smiled. "That's nice of you."

Derek looked askance at the rest of the work site. It was clearing out quickly but wasn't nearly empty enough for him to sneak a kiss.

"But really, Derek, it's not necessary." Thea took a step closer to him. "You should go home and get some rest."

"Ah, but that big empty house."

"Who said it'd be empty?" Thea asked suggestively. *Maybe I'm rubbing off on her a little bit, too.* "I'm going to stay. But if you want you can go ahead, and I'll meet you."

Thea sighed. "That's ridiculous."

"Well, we're already a little behind on the—"

"No, it's ridiculous you think I'm going to go wait for you at your house while you're here working. I'll stay and help."

Derek's eyes widened. "Really?"

"Why are you saying that like it's so hard to believe I might help you out?" she said with a coy smile.

"No, Thea."

"*No, Thea,*" she echoed.

Derek laughed and scratched his head. "You're making it really hard not to kiss you right now."

"In front of all these people."

"Would be bad."

Thea smiled devilishly. "Right."

If he could throw caution to the wind completely, he would. But he had a job to keep. They both did. And with how ill-tempered Tim had been lately about the project, neither of them wanted to cross him.

"So." Thea crossed to the worktable where the last few sprinkler mechanisms sat. "Show me. What do I need to do?"

With Thea's help, Derek got the sprinklers installed in no time. She was a fast learner and a diligent worker. He had expected nothing less.

And, since they were there, the work site empty, the two decided that they might as well work on getting the timer hooked up, too. Then all he and the visuals team would have to do the next day was bury the pipes and move on to the next project.

"Okay, station three runs to zone three, and station four runs to zone five," Thea read off her notes.

"Why does four run to five?"

"I don't know, that's what you told me."

Derek frowned. "I'll have to rework that."

She smiled at him. "You're tired."

"It's been a long day."

She patted the ground beside her. "Come sit."

Derek plopped down on the ground and surveyed the garden. To an outsider's eye, it would have looked like a wreck. But to the creators, it was exactly where it needed to be. He sighed, the peaceful silence of the park settling over him.

Thea slipped her hand around his bicep and looked up at him. "We're alone."

He smiled to himself. "Yeah. We are."

She rested her chin on his shoulder. "Hi."

Derek turned to look at her. Her severe cheekbones weren't so severe when she was looking up at him with doe eyes. "Hi." He kissed her forehead softly.

"Mm," she sighed. "That feels nice."

"You're really letting me do this here?"

"We're alone, aren't we?"

Derek scanned the scenery. Yes, they were alone. Even though they were outside, it was no different than the way they kissed behind the curtains of his house. Someday, he thought, he wanted to kiss her with the windows open. In a way that people could see. "There are some squirrels watching, I think."

Thea laughed. "Well, let them watch. Maybe they're jealous."

He kissed her on the lips softly. "Hey, Thea."

"What, Derek?"

There were so many thoughts inside him bubbling to come out. Any of them could ruin the happiness he'd found here with Thea. He would rather have her in this capacity than not at all. He just wasn't sure how long that would last. "I want to play for you sometime."

Thea lifted her eyebrows in confusion.

"My guitar. I want to play guitar for you. Someday." She smiled. "Really?"

"Yeah, I've never really played for anyone. Well, except Zoe."

"I'm so jealous of her for that."

His heart skipped a beat. "I thought maybe—not today. I'm not ready today."

"That's okay."

"But someday soon, maybe I can play for you."

Thea grinned. "I'd love to listen."

It wasn't the thing he *really* wanted to say. But it was a start. His guitar playing was something he kept close to his heart. The song he'd written for her even closer. Perhaps, once the song was ready, then he would be ready to lay everything on the line for her.

Thea touched his cheek and kissed him before nuzzling her face into his shoulder. "You need a shower."

"So do you."

She got to her feet and gave him her hand. "Maybe we should take one together. To save water."

Derek let Thea help him to his feet. "I think that's a great plan."

Thea didn't let go of his hand once they were standing. Silently, palm to palm, they walked to the parking lot, breaking only when they heard the whine of an electric car zipping down the street.

One day, she won't be a distraction, Derek thought. *One day she'll be my whole world. And I don't care how long it takes.*

Chapter Nine

Kissing goodbye was one of the least favorite parts of Thea's day. Which was funny considering she would see Derek not even half an hour later when they were back on the job at Centennial Park. But it wasn't solely the goodbye, it was what it represented. Like turning off a switch, the kiss indicated that their little dalliance only existed behind closed doors.

And Thea was starting not to like that anymore.

Shocking to no one but her. Although the only other people who knew about the affair were Zoe and Marty.

The last time she'd seen Zoe was over the weekend for dinner, and Thea had disclosed to her friend that she wasn't sure how much longer she could keep up this tryst.

"You're kind of over it, huh?" Zoe asked, lips down-turned.

"No, no. The opposite. I'm afraid if I keep going, I won't be able to stop."

Marty was sitting at the table without saying a word but couldn't help but smile when Thea said that.

"You have something you want to say, Marty?" Thea called him out.

His eyes widened in surprise. "Me? No. No, not at all."

Zoe and Thea exchanged a look. "What's your opinion? I think we'd both like to know."

"I'm just an old man, you don't want to hear that."

Thea resisted rolling her eyes. She hated when Marty played the old man card. Yes, he was over a decade older than his new girlfriend, but he wasn't old, and it certainly didn't bear pointing out on a regular basis.

"But if you ask me— Which you aren't asking me, but—" Marty cleared his throat. "Nothing is worth giving up that feeling. Does that make sense?"

"Aw, honey," Zoe cooed.

Thea would normally feel her stomach turn at that, but this time it didn't. "I can't lose my job, Marty."

"Sure you can. You can work at the diner! Both of you."

Thea laughed.

"He's serious! Right? You're serious."

"Of course!"

Thea couldn't stop laughing. Not because the idea was ludicrous—which it was, but only a little bit—but because she actually was entertaining the thought. What if she and Derek risked everything to be together? They could work at the diner. At least they had each other.

This thought had weighed on Thea's mind for a little under a week. It was interesting in theory, but in practice, psychotic. No way could she give up the only job in

Cloverton that was a fit for her skills to be with a man who'd been her nemesis for nearly a year.

Still, though. Each kiss goodbye inched her closer to that reality.

That all changed the morning after the sprinklers were put in place.

Thea always left five minutes before Derek, so they didn't arrive from the same direction at the same time. So she made it to the worksite first.

Immediately, she could tell something was wrong.

Tim Tate's truck was parked haphazardly in a spot and there was a commotion she could hear all the way from the parking lot. Thea shot out of her car and ran to see what the matter was.

When she laid eyes on the site, her heart sank.

The sprinklers had gone off. And from the looks of it, they had been on all night. Flowerbeds were flooded. Plants had keeled over, root systems drowned, and moats between the cobblestones on the paths.

"For God's sake, someone shut it off!" she heard Tim yell.

Hamilton sprinted past her, followed by Rita. Thea was frozen to her spot, watching the chaos unfold, long enough that she didn't move an inch until Derek appeared at her side.

He was slack-jawed, staring straight ahead. The sprinklers were off now, and Tim had retreated to the trailer, cursing up a storm. What remained was a manmade marshland. "What happened?"

"The sprinklers. They were on all night."

"*What?*"

"I'm just guessing."

"How did that happen?"

Thea and Derek exchanged a look. They might not have known *how* it happened. But they knew they had something to do with it.

"We should check it out," Thea said.

"Yeah. We should."

The two of them approached the mess, water rushing down the walk, wetting the bottoms of their shoes.

"God, this is a mess." Her mind was racing. Funds would have to be allocated from the budget to fix this. A public works grant wasn't going to cover the damage. Or the time it would take to drain the flowerbeds and salvage what they could.

This was the worst possible time to be distracted.

Derek approached a plot of feather reeds that was miraculously standing high. "Well, it's a good thing so many of these plants are resilient."

Thea sighed solemnly. "Yeah."

"Hey."

Her gaze found Derek's. She immediately felt comforted by his steady brown gaze.

"We're going to fix it," he said tenderly.

"It's such a mess, Derek."

"We're going to fix it, Thea. Me and you. Promise."

All at once, she imagined years stretching ahead of them full of tenderness. She could imagine retreating to his arms in tears if she needed comfort, or his touch if she was sick. More than that, Thea could picture him as the sweetest father the world might ever know. The image of big, burly Derek bouncing a delicate little baby on his shoulder sent her head swimming.

"All right?" Derek urged her for an answer.

Thea nodded. "All right."

The visuals team spent the morning building drainage to guide the water from the flowerbeds and onto the pavement. This was only a temporary fix as it was clear that if a horrible storm were to hit the garden, the drainage system was insufficient.

"We need to think about adding more topsoil," Rita suggested.

"Maybe we can talk with the public garden about their compost program. That could create a symbiotic relationship with less upkeep," Derek added.

They both looked to Thea. Her face still hadn't regained color since she walked onto the site that morning. "Sounds good," she said.

Little did she know things were about to go from bad to worse.

"*Thea! Derek!*" Tim shouted from the trailer. "In the office. Now!"

The two lovers didn't move for a long moment. Thea couldn't help but think that Tim knew. Why else would he be calling them in? Yes, she was in charge of running the day-to-day and, yes, Derek was the point person on the visuals team. That was cause enough to call them into the office for a disaster such as this.

Still, though. Something didn't sit well in Thea's gut.

"Yeesh! What'd you do to him?" Rita asked. "Besides the flowerbeds, of course."

"Oh, God," Thea moaned.

Derek tapped her on the arm. "It's okay. Let's just go."

They walked to the office trailer, Derek a foot behind her, as if he was trying to put distance between them. Thea knew that wouldn't work. If Tim knew, Tim knew.

Inside the trailer, Tim was clicking on his laptop furiously, his face redder than a tomato. "Close the door."

Derek did so even though the office became a stuffy hotbox with the door closed.

"Sit."

Thea didn't dare look at Derek as they both sunk into folding chairs across from Tim at the card table.

Tim let them stew in their silence for what felt like an eternity. "Well, this is a fucking shitshow."

"We can make it up," Thea said softly. "With some overtime and—"

"Oh, you better believe we're making it up. We don't have an inch of wiggle room. We are opening the park in a week if it kills me. Or, not me, but *you*," Tim sneered.

Derek cut in. "Tim, this isn't Thea's fault. It's mine. I wanted to have the sprinklers done last night like I promised you, and I must have cut some corners. I'm sorry."

She wished she could grab his hand and thank him for defending her.

"You know, Derek, in any other universe that might have been an acceptable answer, but I'm afraid that's not going to cut." Tim glared between them. "You think you've been slick, huh?"

Thea's stomach dropped.

"I knew something weird was going on when you two weren't going at it like cats and dogs. Actually, I knew it when you started showing up on time," Tim said, jabbing his finger toward Derek.

"W-what are you talking about?" Thea asked. Maybe she could salvage this.

Tim smiled; no one had ever looked so evil. "You two really think I'm an idiot, huh?"

"Tim, that's not—"

Abruptly, Tim turned his computer around. It was paused CCTV footage of the job site.

Right in the center was the blurry, yet unmistakable, image of Derek and Thea. Side by side on the grass. Entangled.

"Well?" Tim asked when neither Thea nor Derek broke the silence.

"Where did you get this?" Derek asked softly.

"I keep cameras on the site, especially when we are leaving materials behind."

Thea had had no idea about this. She thought she was really making headway at Tate. Turned out she was as much in the dark as anyone else.

"So naturally, I come to find the site all fucked up, I'm going to check the cameras, see if there was anyone tampering with our stuff, and lo and behold! I don't need to look an inch further."

"How is this proof of anything?" Thea inquired.

"Distractions, Thea, dear. You two are distractions for each other," Tim hissed.

Thea looked down at Derek's knee. One of his broad hands was clutching the knee of his denim jeans. She wished she could reach out and grab him. Comfort him.

"How long has this been going on?"

Silence.

"Tim—" Thea began, raising her chin. She could do it. She could tell him the truth. She and Derek were more than friends. And she wasn't willing to give him up.

Except Derek beat her to the punch. "Just a couple of weeks. It's casual. Doesn't mean anything. And won't be a problem in the future, I assure you."

More like a punch to the gut. Thea looked straight ahead as if she'd been slapped in the face.

"Well, that's all well and good for the future, but *what* are we doing about *the flooded flowerbeds*?" Tim demanded.

"We'll handle it," Derek reassured again. "I promise. Once it's dried out, we can revive a lot of the flora and fauna we already have. We have some leftover sod an—"

Thea zoned out as Derek walked Tim through all the steps his team was going to take to fix the flooding issue. Her heart had been broken only moments ago. No. *Obliterated*. She never anticipated that gentle, kind Derek would have been capable of such carnage. And yet here she was, feeling like she'd been skinned alive right in front of her boss.

She'd never known Derek cared that much about his job. In fact, between the two of them, she had imagined he'd be the first to want to give that up for her.

How wrong she was.

"It won't happen again," she whispered.

The two men stopped talking and looked at her.

"What'd you say?" Tim questioned.

Thea raised her gaze and looked at Derek. The man whose bed she had been sharing. The man she'd grown to adore in such a short period of time. The man who'd made her think that things might eventually be different.

In an instant, he'd betrayed her.

"It won't happen again, is what I said," Thea repeated, looking Derek directly in the eye.

Derek flinched.

"Well, it better not. Or else, someone is losing their job. If not both of you. So get your act together. And *fix it*."

"Right away, Mr. Tate," Thea said in a monotone.

Then, without another word, she got up out of her seat and left the trailer.

This was as good a reason as any to never expose her heart to anyone again.

Chapter Ten

"You want to try working on fingerpicking again?" Zoe asked.

Derek grunted. He almost didn't come to this lesson at all. It was too embarrassing to face Zoe. He knew she must know what had happened at work the week before.

However, he'd gotten his four-thirty Tuesday lesson reserved months ago. He'd be foolish to cancel. Especially at the last minute.

"Sure. I guess."

"'Blackbird'. Go for it."

Derek began picking the opening notes for 'Blackbird' by The Beatles. They'd been working on this tune for much longer than Derek would have liked. His wide-tipped fingers made it difficult sometimes to strum a single string at a time and, consequently, he didn't enjoy practicing it. Which, in turn, meant he never got much better at it.

Right before he was supposed to come in with the lyrics, he stopped. "Sorry, I just … I can't do it today."

Zoe's forehead scrunched together. All Derek could see was pity in her eyes. She must think he was pathetic. "You okay?"

He half-laughed. "Come on, Zoe. You don't have to pretend not to know."

Zoe's shoulders fell slightly.

"Maybe it wasn't a great idea for me to come here today. I thought it would make me feel better, but—"

"Derek, when you're here, you're just a student playing guitar. I know it's weird because Thea is my friend, but that's all that it's ever been, right?"

Derek looked at the redhead and shrugged. "I guess so."

"We don't have to play that song if you don't want to. In fact, we don't have to play at all." Zoe smiled. "I don't want you to run away from me, because you think I have something against you."

He muttered his thanks.

"Besides, how could I? None of this is either of your faults."

Derek eyed his guitar teacher, softly running his hand over the outside of his guitar. *I shouldn't ask, but I have to know*. "Has she said anything about me?"

Zoe shook her head sadly. "But that shouldn't make you feel bad. That's the way Thea is. She's either spilling her guts or not saying a word. Not the healthiest way to be, but—"

"She hasn't said a thing to me since Tim found out. Not one word." Derek closed his eyes, remembering how earlier that day, he'd merely muttered "Excuse me" to get past her and she hadn't even looked up. "She isn't even rude to me. I mean, I'd rather have that than nothing at all."

Zoe chuckled. "That's sweet."

"It doesn't feel sweet. It feels lame."

She leaned back in her child-sized chair. Zoe held guitar lessons in the music room at Cloverton Elementary School. The student got the teacher's chair, and Zoe sat in the tiny chair. It was awkward, but that's how it went. "You know, Derek, all Zoe has really ever had to count on in her adult life is her work."

"What do you mean?"

"I mean her parents are always doing their own thing now that she doesn't live at home so she can't always count on them. Her friends are..." Zoe trailed off and looked away. "Well, I haven't always been the best friend. Not around a lot. And now I'm in a relationship, so she probably always feels like she's a lower priority. And she's never had a boyfriend for longer than a few months. She's always had to rely on herself. A job, to her, is the most accountable thing a person can have. So when it's threatened, *she's* being threatened. You get what I mean?"

Derek sighed. "Yeah, I get it."

"But it's stupid."

"You said it, not me."

Zoe considered Derek carefully. "Thea said you were the one who admitted to what you guys had going on. And that you made it sound really trivial."

Derek's eyes widened. "I had to say that. For Tim. Did she— Did she take me seriously?"

"I don't know for a fact. I'm just guessing, but—"

"Oh, God. Oh no. No, I didn't— Shit."

"Hey, relax." Zoe touched his shoulder. "It was a misunderstanding. That's okay."

Derek shook his head. "I never wanted to make her feel bad, though. Ever." Now it all made sense. The way she avoided him at work and the way she looked through him rather than at him.

He'd broken her heart when all he'd wanted to do was keep it safe.

"How do you feel about her? I mean, if things hadn't played out like this, would you have wanted to keep seeing her?"

"Yes, absolutely." Derek hesitated and then admitted slowly, "I fell for her. You know?"

Zoe smiled. "I get it."

"I knew we couldn't keep going like we were for too long. But we also couldn't be anything more. It was complicated."

They were quiet.

"I wrote a fucking song about her."

"Derek! You wrote a song about her?! That's so exciting!"

"No, it's not exciting. It's bad. The lyrics are cliché and trivial and—"

Zoe put her hands to her cheeks. "You wrote her a song!" "That's so sweet!"

"It's not like that, it's bad. I didn't know what else to do."

"Derek, you *like* her. You really like her."

Derek closed his eyes and grunted in frustration. Yes, wasn't that painfully obvious at this point? "We barely know each other."

"You've worked together for a year. That isn't barely knowing each other."

This was true. Even though they had bristled against one another from the start, he'd watched her work for almost a year. She was driven, a perfectionist, and yet she wasn't afraid to get her hands dirty.

He wanted a woman unafraid to get her hands dirty. That kind of woman knew where she came from.

"Just because you haven't had an opportunity to get to know one another doesn't mean you don't *know* each other at all. Besides, I think you know Thea a bit better than you're letting on."

"Maybe."

"What would you do if you knew you couldn't lose?"

Derek opened his eyes. "Wow. That's a big question."

"Well, I'm asking you. What would you do if you knew that nothing could possibly go wrong? That everything would go to plan."

He thought for a moment. "I'd get her back."

"Okay."

"And our job wouldn't care. Or that's not going to happen. So, I guess I'd quit my job."

"Wow, that's a lot of good information. You'd quit your job for Thea?"

Derek smiled goofily at that. "I'd quit my job for Thea."

"You're insane! I love it."

Derek didn't feel like it was insane though. It felt right. He'd given up on her too quickly, been forced to put their relationship into review before he was ready. He didn't know if they were forever yet. But he knew that if he didn't try, he'd live his whole life regretting what could have been with Thea Winton.

"You have to tell her."

"What?! No. I can't. At least not until we're done with Centennial Park. Maybe then will make sense but—"

"Dude, you're really gonna wait because some guy said you're not allowed to? What are you, chicken?"

Derek's stomach dropped. "No."

"Sounds kinda chicken to me."

There was something to what Zoe was saying. Why should Derek live his life under the thumb of some other man? Shouldn't he be free to do as he pleased? To pursue the things he wanted without anyone stepping in his way? That's what his ancestors would want from him. That's what nature intended. "Fine. I'll do it."

"Perfect. You can sing her your song."

Derek's eyes widened in alarm. "Um. No way."

"Oh, come on. It's so romantic."

He shook his head. "It would be romantic if it was good and I was talented, but neither of those things are true."

"You're always selling yourself short, Derek. Stop that! You're a great guitar player and you've got a nice voice. You just have to take the risk to be heard."

Derek sat back in his seat and tapped his fingers against the body of his guitar. The thought of revealing his feelings to Thea in a song was cringe ... beyond cringe. However, while the lyrics were cliché, they did express exactly how he felt about her. His hazy-eyed girl. "If she hates my guts, could you imagine anything more mortifying than hearing a song about how much a guy likes you?"

Zoe twisted her lips together. "Fair point, although I really don't think that's going to happen."

Maybe not. But Derek wasn't yet willing to risk it. "I'll play it for you. How about that?"

She clapped her hands together. "I'd like nothing more."

"But you can't face me."

"Fine."

"And you have to be honest. If it's bad. You tell me. Okay?"

Zoe flipped around in her chair. "Just play it."

Derek took a deep breath and then played it. He fumbled some of the fingering and flipped some of the lyrics around, but when all was said and done, Zoe turned back to him, tears in her eyes. "That was beautiful. That was Thea."

Chapter Eleven

Since having to give up Derek, every day at work had been torture for Thea. And Somehow Derek kept getting hotter. She wasn't sure if that was the reality, or it was because he was something she couldn't have. Nevertheless, every time he was in her field of vision, she had to look away.

It was embarrassing overall. Especially the way Tim treated her after the news came to light. "You were my number one, Thea," he said disappointedly. "I thought I could count on you."

She had been scrounging around for her dignity every day since. Tim had raised the bar for her to reach, and she was determined to get back in his good graces.

The grand opening was Saturday at four in the evening. It would be an amazing event filled with music, food, carnival games, and shopping from local vendors. Zoe would be leading her music class in a rousing rendition of ...

something... on recorders. Other, more seasoned acts, were also on the schedule.

However, the landscapers were still behind. Specifically, the visuals team, which was to be expected after the flooding. To make matters worse, Thea couldn't lend her extra hands to help them. She hadn't spoken to Derek since they were found out and it would be too awkward.

There was one way she thought she could be of help, though.

Thea rolled a cart with flats of violets over to the flowerbeds. She had anticipated simply dropping them off, and then sneaking away to deal with some other fire that needed putting out, but Rita spotted her with catlike intensity.

"What are those for?" she demanded.

"The violets. For the flowerbeds."

"Guys! We got the violets!"

Thea started to back away, not wanting to be seen, but was too slow. Derek emerged from behind a hedge he was trimming, sweat on his brow and his hair twisted into a bun on the back of his head. He looked at the cart of flowers and then to Thea for an explanation.

"They're dog violets," she explained. "I thought you were right. They made more sense than the common ones. If we were going to have to put them in the beds at all."

Call it a peace offering, but Thea did think it was their best bet to stick to the contract and also protect the rest of the plants from being overrun.

Derek nodded. "Thanks, Thea."

"You're welcome," she said. Or did she say it? She wasn't sure. All she cared about was getting out of there as quickly as possible. In fact, she needed a break. Perhaps an iced coffee from The Coffee Nut was in order. She could do a big coffee run. That would take a long time. That would keep her away from Derek for enough time to calm herself down.

Thea rushed out to the parking lot, keys in hand, but stopped when she heard Derek call out after her, "Thea! Wait."

She stopped, a few steps away from her car, unwilling to turn around. Would she be a total asshole if she hopped in and pretended like she hadn't heard him? The answer would be yes. Still, though, she was halfway willing to risk it.

"Wait up. I need to talk to you."

Thea turned, squeezing her eyes shut. *If you can't see him, you can't remember how much you want him.* "Derek, we aren't supposed to be alone together. "

"That was never a part of the rules."

Thea blinked her eyes open and looked down at their feet. "What do you want?"

"Can I talk to you? Would you let me?"

Thea took a deep breath. "Not here. Behind your truck." For some reason, it felt safer to stand behind his truck than next to her tiny sedan.

"Yeah, that's fine."

The two of them walked over to the truck and stood at the end of the bed.

"What do you need to talk to me about?" Thea asked softly.

"Would you look at me for a second?"

The corners of her mouth tightened. "I can't."

Derek hesitated. "Okay."

"Just say what you need to say. I'm not going anywhere."

Derek leaned on the back of the truck. "This is bullshit. We're adults, Thea. We shouldn't be told what we can and can't do."

She laughed meekly. "Well, in a perfect world, I'd have to agree but—"

"Fuck that. I mean ..." his voice softened. "I'm miserable, Thea."

I'm miserable too, she thought.

"The fact that the only thing standing between me and you right now is my job is killing me. Because I—" Derek stopped. "Please look at me."

His pleading was impossible to ignore. Thea raised her eyes to his and immediately felt like she might pass out. He looked so beautiful. His caramel skin, his dark hair and eyebrows, his strong jaw. *Beautiful*.

"I want to be with you."

Her heart expanded.

"And I don't care if I don't have a job because of it."

Hearing him say this was ludicrous. Truly insane. They had been "together" for three weeks. Now he wanted to give up his livelihood for her? It wasn't that Thea didn't want to believe it. It's that she couldn't. What man would think her that special? "Derek, it's not that simple."

"We can do this," he said urgently, gesturing back toward the park. "We can start our own company. We can do this kind of work for ourselves."

"Are you crazy? Neither of us has enough experience."

"That's not true. You have the creativity and organizational skills. I have the technical know-how. It's simple."

Sadly, Thea didn't believe she was capable of something like that. "Derek ..."

"Don't say 'can't', Thea. You're way too good for 'can't'," he said firmly. "If I'm not the man you want, then fine. But don't tell me you can't do that. Because you can. I know you can."

Tears welled in Thea's eyes. All she wanted was to get in her car and go grab an iced coffee and be alone for ten minutes, so she didn't have to deal with all of this. It was too much. "Derek, I don't know."

"I want to be with you. Do you want to be with me?"

"I—"

"That's the only question you need to answer."

"Derek, I—"

He grabbed her shoulders. Thea didn't fight back for a second. It was just so good to be touched by him again. "It's just yes or no."

Thea shook her head in confusion.

And against his better judgment, Derek leaned in and kissed her. Hard, firm, unyielding. This was his position. He was here. He was in it. And he was willing to risk it all.

Thea felt like a coward.

Because she was not ready to risk it all.

Derek drew away. "Well?"

Thea blinked, tears rolling down her face. "Derek, I don't—"

"Do you think I'm stupid or something?" Tim's voice interrupted.

Thea and Derek leapt apart. Without knowing it, Tim had snuck up on them from beside the truck and had his hands on his hips like an old schoolmarm.

"What the fuck is the matter with you two? Right out in the parking lot? In the middle of the workday?! Where *everyone can see*?"

Thea winced at the decibel of Tim's voice.

"I ought to fire you both on the spot."

Chapter Twelve

Derek insisted that Tim speak to him first.

"Less than a week later and here you are, Derek. I told you not to let it happen again."

Derek smiled sadly. "I know."

"And yet you did."

"Yep."

Tim frowned. "You don't seem the least bit remorseful."

Derek gritted his teeth and took a breath before speaking. "You know, it's funny. I'm not."

His boss scoffed. "What?"

"Yeah. I'm just not sorry."

"Your job is on the line, young man."

"Right. I know. Actually, I'd like to talk to you about that. I'm thinking given the imminent deadline, you're not going to want to try and replace two employees, let alone one. I suggest you keep Thea and let me go."

Tim sat ramrod straight and his jaw dropped. "I don't understand."

"She's more important here anyway. You add another guy onto the visuals job, that's as good as replacing me." Derek didn't feel this in his heart of hearts, but right now, his goal was protecting Thea above all else. "Plus, it's my fault she's in this mess. I pursued her. Not the other way around." *Might as well spice it up. Really sell it.*

"I don't know what to say."

"You don't have to say anything. We can leave it at that."

Tim shook his head. "You're a great worker, Derek. I can't afford to have either of you so distracted."

"I understand."

"I mean, it already created such a problem before—"

"Only a matter of time before it happens again."

"Precisely."

Tim sighed. "You're a great kid."

"Thanks."

"You've done a lot for Tate."

"Thank you."

"Just need to shape up a bit, you know? Take work a bit more seriously than your personal time."

If Derek was willing to fight for his job, he'd be giving Tim a piece of his mind. But he had no use for it. It would only make this harder than it needed to be. "Thanks for the tip."

"Sure, sure."

The two men stared at each other.

"Can I go?" Derek asked.

"Yes, I guess that's best."

"Great."

Derek pushed himself up from his chair and went toward the door. He did this for himself and for Thea. It was up to her if she wanted to take the next step.

"And Derek?"

"Yes, Mr. Tate."

"Try to go quietly, please."

Derek smiled bitterly. "Of course, Mr. Tate."

Derek slammed the door behind him and let out a loud sigh. Around him, the world was quiet. It was always sort of funny to him how something life-changing could happen and yet the world didn't seem to take notice. Or perhaps it was taking the most amount of notice. Going on and accommodating space for whatever was going to happen next.

"What happened?"

Derek turned to see Thea at the end of the trailer, waiting nervously.

"What do you think?" he asked with a soft smirk.

"Guess it's my turn, huh?"

Derek shook his head and started to walk past her.

"Derek?"

"I have to go, Thea."

She followed at his heels. "Derek, what's going on?"

He stopped and turned to face her. "I'm leaving. I'm fired."

"And now me."

"No. I'm fired. And you're not."

Thea's jaw dropped. "That jackass! That's— That's so unfair! How could he—"

"Thea, that's what I asked him to do. I get let go so you can stay."

She blinked, her blue eyes still wet with the tears he'd made fall only twenty minutes earlier. "What? Why would you do that?"

"Because this job means more to you than it does to me."

Thea frowned. "I can't help but feel like that's meant to be an insult."

"No, that's not—" Derek sighed. "Look. You care. You care a lot. And Tate needs you more than me. I'm replaceable. You're not."

"That's not true."

He wasn't willing to do the runaround argument. It wasn't going to help anybody. He'd made his choice and, given the way she'd reacted to his declaration, she had, too. "Just don't let them push you around, okay? You're better than them."

"Derek, you can't go," she whispered and took a step toward him. "You can't—"

Derek stepped back, away from her reach. "I promised I'd go quietly." He could see the space between them, a huge abyss that seemed unbridgeable. "Forget what I said, okay?"

"What?"

"I was— It was silly." It wasn't silly. Not really. "I don't want you to feel bad or beholden to—"

"I do feel bad. Derek, we both did this. I should leave too. I should be fired."

"Thea, if you were to leave with me, it would end up bad for both of us."

She pursed her lips together as if she'd eaten something sour. "You really changed your mind in just twenty minutes?"

His mind hadn't changed. But she did not return his passion or adamance. His balloon was deflated. "It's not that simple."

"Or it wasn't real to begin with."

"If that's what you want to believe."

Thea looked away and then back at Derek. "I guess take care."

"You, too. Best of luck. You'll do great."

Thea lingered another moment.

What did she want him to say? Declare his love all over again after she'd denied him the catharsis of loving him back? There was nothing left to be said.

As soon as she understood that, Thea turned away and walked slowly back toward Centennial Park.

Derek let out a sigh of relief. Or was it disappointment? Regardless, he climbed into his truck and drove off in the direction of home. It was time to rest. Time to forget.

Except how could he? When every corner of his house had somehow managed to attach itself to a memory of Thea. In the front hall, he remembered tripping over her shoes. In the kitchen, he'd made her try the sautéed nettles and, to her surprise, she liked them. In the living room, they'd sat on the couch together and marveled at how they'd ended up there.

"I thought you hated me," Thea had said.

"I thought *you* hated *me*," he'd replied.

She'd smiled. "No, I just didn't know how to talk to you because you were cute."

"Are you saying you were bullying me because you thought I was cute?"

"Listen, I'm not proud of it, but—"

Derek had tackled her, peppering kisses across her face and chest, reveling in her shrill giggling.

How was he going to forget all those wonderful little snippets of their time together?

Sleep. That's what I need. Sleep.

Derek lugged himself upstairs. If he wanted to sleep, that meant he'd have to shower before getting into bed. And, unfortunately, there were memories of Thea there too. A handful of times the two of them negotiated who got to be under the showerhead, grabbing onto each other for balance, laughing and kissing, and on at least one occasion, having amazing sex up against the shower wall.

You'll have amazing sex again, he told himself. Did he believe it? Well, not yet. Someday he would. He hoped.

After showering, he crawled into bed and shut his eyes.

But Thea was there too. More literally than every other place. There were strands of her hair buried in the sheets.

"God fucking *damn it*," he growled, burying his face in his pillow. He'd washed the sheets. How was she still here? Why wouldn't she leave him alone?

Derek lay awake for hours, terrified that Thea Winton would never leave his head and he would be doomed to want her for the rest of his life.

There were perhaps worse existences, but there were certainly better.

He finally fell asleep when he chose to believe he would be alone forever. And that it was for the best.

Whether he believed that, well, that was a concern for a different day.

Chapter Thirteen

"You know, after the flowerbed situation, I didn't think you could do it, Thea," Tim said, putting his hand on her shoulder. "But you did."

If that wasn't the most backhanded compliment Thea had ever received...

Thea and Tim were standing at the entrance to the new addition to Centennial Park. It looked glorious. Between the brand-new band shell and the shiny cobblestone pathways, it was finally fit for all of Cloverton to see. The crowning jewel, though, was the prairie-like landscaping, full of native Illinois flowers and patches of a look-alike to the native violets that only Thea and the visuals team knew weren't the real deal.

It made her feel hollow inside to look at it. She was celebrating this achievement on her own. No amount of compliments from Tim could make her feel whole again, especially now that she knew his true colors.

The violets in particular broke her heart. She'd had to help plant them. It was almost like a curse, popping the scentless purple flowers into their loamy homes. Now, they lined the walkways, their faces taunting her. "Remember what you gave up? Was it worth it?"

"I want you to do the welcome speech," Tim said, shaking her shoulder a bit too forcefully. "You earned it."

Thea shook her head. "I couldn't possibly. I wouldn't know what to say."

"Oh, just talk about how much the park means to Cloverton, what parts of the community it's going to reach, yada yada yada. You'd be better at it than me, believe me."

Tim was, at the very least, right about that. It was clear he couldn't give a flying fuck about the town of Cloverton at all. He was here to run a business and take their money. Nothing more.

Her boss checked his watch and cleared his throat. "You have an hour before the ceremony. You'll come up with something." Then, with a final pat on the back, Tim walked off, leaving Thea alone to look at what she'd accomplished.

It wasn't worth it, she thought.

Yes, the landscaping was some of her finest work. There were hiccups along the way, but she'd done it. The swath of prairie flowers, the simple yet serviceable bandshell that was already booked out through Halloween for weekend concerts and performances, the maze of paths that would lead anyone looking for quiet to peace.

None of it was worth Derek losing his job. More than that, it wasn't worth Thea losing Derek.

In the days since he'd walked off the site, she'd tried to call him. She never actually dialed his number. But she'd tried to. Sitting with her phone in her lap, finger hovering over the call button, never getting the confidence to do it.

She didn't know what she was going to get. Was he going to be the Derek behind the truck with her, desperate for her to give in to her feelings? Or the one after being fired, martyring himself so everything could remain the same for her?

It was whiplash. Thea wasn't sure she could handle more, especially if she wanted to remain sane and finish the project.

Now, though, the project was done. And Tim had shoved another task off onto her that he didn't want to do.

She couldn't do this alone. She needed Zoe.

"If anyone blows into their recorder one more time," Zoe shouted over the swarm of children peppering the grass, "I am taking it, and you will have to mime a recorder through the performance."

There was a final toot from a recorder and then silence.

She pointed into the crowd of kids and narrowed her eyes. "Next one, I'm serious."

"Hey," Thea said, approaching the group.

"Thank you for being here," Zoe breathlessly replied, grabbing Thea by the arm. "I think I'm about to lose my sanity with these recorders."

Thea giggled. "I think you're just nervous."

"Of course I'm nervous! We're performing first, and we're playing 'The Star-Spangled Banner!' I want to bring a tear to the eye of everyone at the bandshell," Zoe said. Her expression changed suddenly. "What's wrong?"

"Huh?"

"Your face is all limp and sad. What's going on?"

"Hasn't my face been limp and sad for, like, two weeks now?"

"Yes, but today is supposed to be happy! Today you accomplished something. So what's going on?"

Thea sighed and looked askance at the kids.

"Hey! I'm going over here for a second—" Zoe announced to the children, pointing to a big oak tree. "I will be listening for any recorders piping when they shouldn't be making a peep!"

The group of kids all laughed.

"You've been warned."

The two women walked over to the oak tree, Zoe's eyes glancing back at the children every now and again, fearful of hearing a recorder playing out of turn. "Okay, what's going on?"

"I'm supposed to make the welcome speech."

"That's great!"

"It's not great, because I have no idea what to say. Tim sprung this on me like five minutes ago."

Zoe grimaced. "I hate that guy."

"Yeah, me, too." Thea had never admitted that out loud. And it felt really good.

"Well, you'll think of something. Just talk about the park and what it means for all of us. How the flowers represent going back to our roots." Zoe snapped.

"That's not half bad."

"Listen, I'm clever in a pinch."

Thea went silent.

"It's not about any of that, though, is it?"

Tucking a curl of hair behind her ear, Thea looked off across the park. "I can't stop thinking about him. I'm miserable."

Zoe sighed. "I know, Thea."

"There's nothing to celebrate today. Because Derek should be here. He should have been able to finish this out with us. And I'm supposed to give some speech about how amazing the park is when I'm the one who got him fired."

"You didn't get him fired. He made choices too."

Thea swallowed. "But I knew it was dangerous. I should have stuck to my guns. I shouldn't have let him cloud my judgement or—"

"*Enough*, Thea," Zoe snapped. "Is that what your life is all about? Being *Employee of the Month* every month until you die?"

Thea's eyes widened. It was a little harsh, but Zoe wasn't wrong.

"Your job isn't going to keep you warm at night."

"It keeps the heat on."

"Stop being a contrarian! You know what I'm saying!"

Thea did. But being contrarian protected her from the truth of her emotions. Emotions were subjective, especially when they involved other people. Her job could be objective when she was performing at her best. Is that what she wanted from life? Not really. But it wasn't as scary as the subjectivity and vulnerability it took to involve another person in her world.

"Derek got fired because of you. He wanted to protect you. If that doesn't prove how much he cares about you, then maybe you have a heart of stone."

Thea gasped. "I don't have a heart of stone!"

"Okay, then act like it! Get the stick out of your ass and tell that man how you feel about him because he's pretty much done everything he can to make it known how he feels about you."

Thea harrumphed. "I came over here for advice about my speech."

"Well, I'm done letting you sabotage your own life, Thea. You're great at what you do. There will be other jobs." Zoe then smiled softly. "But there are not a lot of Dereks out there."

This is what Thea had asked for. She wanted someone, just as Zoe had someone, just as it seemed everyone in Cloverton had someone.

Derek was her someone.

And she'd pushed him away.

"You'll do great at the speech. Whatever you say. I don't even think most people will really be listening if I'm honest," Zoe continued. "Just say what you feel. And then—" Her eyes sparkled. "You have to go find him.

Thea threw her arms around her friend and hugged her tightly. "Thank you."

"Oh." Zoe hugged her back. "You're going to make me cry."

Thea hugged tighter. She knew exactly what she had to do.

The benches for the bandshell were full. People had congregated on picnic blankets. Some people who were passing through walking their dogs stopped to listen.

It was time. Thea was ready to be brave.

At three on the dot, she approached the mic at the front of the bandshell. She had not taken notes or written anything down. She was just going to say what she felt.

The people of Cloverton applauded her and she flushed. At the back of the crowd, Tim gave her a thumbs up and then returned to tapping on his phone.

You're really selling this whole "I care" thing, Tim, Thea thought. Then, she shook him off. Tim didn't matter. All that mattered was saying what she meant so she could get out of there and find Derek.

"Good afternoon," Thea said into the mic. "This is a perfect day to be in the park. I'm so glad we can share it all together."

She scanned the familiar faces in the crowd. Marty and Ella. The Kahns. Olivia and Wes Hooper, both happily paired with their partners.

BY DESIGN   113

"I don't have much to say other than a few thank-yous. First, to the historical preservation committee, namely Alice DePowell, for getting us the grant money to redevelop this part of the park." Thea looked at Alice who was sitting toward the back with her daughter Ginny and Ginny's boyfriend, Ben. The elderly woman waved at Thea sweetly. "Without this money, the south end of Centennial Park would still be in disrepair. Now, it can usher in a new era of community engagement." *You sound like a robot, Thea. Relax.* "Next, I'd like to thank Tate's Landscaping for giving me an opportunity to be a part of this development. And then ..."

Thea trailed off when she caught sight of someone on the outskirts of the celebration. Derek. With his guitar slung over his shoulder.

Thea was quiet for a moment as she stared at him. This wasn't how it was supposed to go. She was supposed to give her speech and then she'd find him, not him finding her. It was all backward.

Fuck the plan. This is what life is giving you, Thea. Are you going to let it pass you by?

"Finally, I'd like to thank Derek Harper, head of our visuals team."

Out of the corner of her eye, she saw Tim's head jerk upward and a scowl appear on his face.

"Without him, there's no way this gorgeous garden would have gotten done. This garden represents our native Illinoisan heritage. What came before us. What thrives without us. While making this garden, Derek not only guided us in how to balance these plants so they could

thrive together, but he salvaged weeds to cook with."
Thea's eyes met Derek. "Make tea with. The way that
nature intended. This garden isn't for us. It's for the land.
And that is thanks to him."

Thea took a deep breath. *Might have just lost my job for
that.* And somehow, that was okay. "All that's left to say is
enjoy. Thank you."

She booked it off the stage in Derek's direction as Zoe's
troupe of recorder players marched on to play.

Derek welcomed her with a curious smile. "Hey."

"Hi," she said breathlessly. "Was that bad? Do you think
people thought that was weird?"

He grinned. "No, it was great. You did a great job,
Thea."

"Oh. Good."

"Thea," Tim growled as he approached the couple.
"What the hell was that?"

Don't back down. This is your moment. "I was saying
what was true."

"What was true? This—" Tim sneered and pointed at
Derek. "He didn't have anything to do with any of this."

"Of course, he did. You were a fool to let him walk
away."

Tim raised an eyebrow. "Are you saying you should have
been fired instead?"

"Maybe. But that doesn't matter now because I quit."

It popped out as easy as breathing. The relief was imme-
diate for Thea. She'd been avoiding the idea for weeks now.
And the moment it was real, she felt free. She should have
quit sooner.

"You quit? Don't be ridiculous!" Tim yelped.

In the background, the recorders played "The Star-Spangled Banner" to varying degrees of success, meaning everyone's attention was rapt and hearing was pierced. They could have this conversation unencumbered by prying ears.

"Thea, you don't have to do that," Derek whispered to her.

But she did. Oh, she definitely did. Thea no longer wanted to be under the thumb of a tyrannical, thoughtless boss. And she no longer wanted her life and choices dictated by a job that truly wouldn't keep her warm at night when Derek—sweet, loving Derek—was right there.

"You two you can have your—" Tim scrambled his fingers around like a child who thought touching girls gave you cooties. "And you can keep your job. You don't have to be dramatic about this."

"Actually, I can't. It doesn't work for me," Thea said. It was time to start fresh. Time to choose what really mattered in her life.

And that was Derek.

Tim looked aghast, unable to respond. Thea wasn't going to give him a chance to talk her out of her decision.

"Thanks for the opportunities, Tim. But I'm done. This was my last job." Thea grabbed Derek's hand. "Come on, let's go.'"

Thea pulled Derek away from the park, relishing the frustrated squeal Tim let out as she left.

"Holy shit, you just did that," Derek murmured in shock.

"I know, I feel like I'm going to pass out," Thea said. There was no room for regret. She didn't have any.

She knew she had made the right choice.

"That was so hot," Derek said, still in shock.

Thea let out a loud laugh. "I'm glad you think so."

They exchanged smiles as they walked, not knowing where they were going but not worried about their destination.

Derek's hand tightened in hers. "Come with me. I want to show you something."

Chapter Fourteen

Derek and Thea walked to the north end of Centennial Park, which was very empty for a Saturday, no doubt due to the celebration at the south end.

This was perfect for Derek's purposes though.

Derek led Thea over to the gazebo and sat her down on the stairs. "I, uh…" He opened his guitar case and removed the acoustic. "I wrote a song for you."

Thea's eyes widened, a smile spreading across her lips. "You wrote a song for me?"

He nodded and settled down on the stairs, guitar on his lap. He held the neck in his hand and let out a sigh. "Sorry, my heart is still pounding."

"It's okay." Thea reached out and took his hand. "There's no rush."

Derek looked at the way her hand folded around his with tenderness. "I thought I was going to have to convince you to listen to me."

"Well, I thought I was going to have to convince *you* to listen to *me*."

He laughed softly. "That makes sense, I guess."

They sat in silence together, the strange silence of Cloverton creating a vacuum that was just for them.

"You shouldn't have quit your job for me," Derek said. "That's ridiculous."

Thea smiled. "Not to me."

"But what are you going to do?"

"Marty offered me a job at Deep Fried Diner. If that's what I have to do to be with you, that's what I have to do."

Derek felt his heart flutter. "You want to be with me?"

Bashfully, Thea looked away. "I mean, if you want to be with me."

"You know I want to."

She shook her head. "Derek, you confessed you wanted to be with me, and then took it away from me within half an hour. I don't know what you want. I need you to tell me again."

Derek nodded. "All right, then. Thea."

"Yes?"

He looked deep into her eyes. The most beautiful woman he'd ever laid eyes on. Maybe even more beautiful first thing in the morning. "I want to give things a go between us. For real. Not sneaking around, not just sex. I want to know every part of you."

Thea's shoulders lifted with her smile. "Oh, my gosh."

Derek laughed. "You're so cute when you're nervous."

Thea giggled excitedly and pressed a kiss to the back of his hand. "Play it for me. Please play it for me."

He'd practiced with Zoe several times by this point, enlisting her for extra lessons in the past week. He'd gotten confident. But he'd never gotten to the point where he could have Zoe look at him while he played. He'd always mess up every time he felt eyes on him.

"It's okay. You can ask her not to look," Zoe said the day before when they were practicing late into the night.

But that felt cowardly, and Derek was tired of cowardice.

No. He wasn't going to have Thea look away from him. Because this song was entirely for her.

Derek cleared his throat. "All right."

Thea dropped her hand from his and gripped the stair beneath her as she watched him prepare.

He positioned his fingers over the right cord, strummed to make sure the guitar was in tune, and when he was sufficiently ready—or ready as he'd ever be—he began to play.

"*Hazy blue. Too easy to get lost in you.*"

Thea smiled brightly.

"*It's too good to be true, but I can't stop. Don't want to stop.*"

Derek worked through the first verse, the chords coming easily, his voice finding strength. And when he got to the chorus, he knew he was home free. "*Accidents aren't always meant to be, but this accident of you and me feels right. So come home with me tonight. Let me get lost in you, my hazy blue.*"

Thea listened with rapt attention, her smile falling, not from sadness or disappointment, but from the shock that he'd been inspired by her to create a beautiful song. Needful and vulnerable. Derek was exposing his whole heart to her. She was prepared to take it with loving, careful hands and hold onto it for as long as he'd let her.

As the final notes faded away, Derek let out a long sigh of relief. He let the strings ring out and then raised his eyes to Thea. "That was terrifying."

"It was amazing."

For some reason, that made him want to cry tears of joy. "Thank you."

"You really wrote that for me?"

"Thea…" Derek put his guitar to the side and slid next to her. He took her hands in his. "I would write thousands of songs for you. Because the way I feel about you scares me. I've never felt this way about anyone." Truly, no one. Not even the ex he had been carrying a torch for, for three years. He couldn't even believe he thought that was real love when he was feeling like this for Thea.

Not that it was love. Or at least, not that he would say it out loud yet. It had only been about a month. That would be crazy, right?

But this whole thing was kind of crazy.

"I want to be with you, Derek," Thea said. "I want to be with you in the light of day."

Derek looked around. Once again, here they were, seeing the light of day, yet no one was around to look at them. To let them know that they had been seen.

Thea wanted to be seen. Derek was going to make that happen.

"Do you trust me?" Derek asked.

Her eyes widened. "Well, I guess I have to."

"You don't have to."

Thea squeezed his hand. "Okay. Yes. Yes, I do."

"Good. Then, first of all—" Derek kissed her deeply on the lips. It had been too long, even though it had barely been a week. He had been yearning for her touch again with his body and soul. This kiss sealed them back together. For good this time. At least he hoped.

When he broke away, Thea looked around in a daze. "How are you so good at that?"

Derek laughed, feeling his cheeks heat up. Then, he got to his feet. "Now, the second part. We're going back."

"What?" Thea asked with wild eyes.

"We're going back to the celebration. You want to be seen, well, that's where everybody is. Let's be seen, Thea."

Thea got to her feet, legs trembling like a newborn foal. "I can't go back there. I just made an amazing exit."

"Fuck Tim. We're going back there together to rub it in his face and let everyone else know that you and I are a thing, right?"

Her eyes were wide.

"We're the real thing, right?" Derek asked nervously. He couldn't handle another rejection. He would surely disintegrate into dust and float away on the wind. That'd be quite a dramatic way to go.

Thankfully, Thea's face brightened. "Yeah. We are." Then, she kissed him with all her might. "Let's go. I want to show you off."

The two of them snuck back to watch the rest of the performances, finding an empty spot that was perfect for just the two of them. They sat hand in hand, not even listening to the music. Just soaking it all in.

People weren't looking at them, at least they weren't staring. But Derek could see the information move through the crowd. The gossipy hair stylist caught sight of them first, then whispered something to the bakery owner, who then told her personal trainer boyfriend, who leaned forward to let the math teacher know, and so on and so on until it seemed like all of Cloverton knew.

And that was how Thea and Derek came to be.

At the end of the concert, everyone dispersed to enjoy food and libations and visit the various booths of Cloverton's stores that were scattered around the park. This was where Thea and Derek really got to show off.

But not before they were cornered by matchmaker of the century, Zoe Redford.

"Oh, my gosh, you two are so cute together," she exclaimed, rushing over with Ella and Marty in tow. "You're even cuter than I could have pictured. Aren't they cute together, honey?"

Marty nodded. "Very cute."

Thea smiled at Marty. She'd been wary of her friend's older boyfriend, but she'd come to adore him over the past month. He was kind and sensitive, and it was clear through the way he treated Thea that he loved Zoe deeply. "Marty, I might need that job you were talking about," she said sheepishly.

"We're always happy to have you, Thea. You too, Derek. By the way, nice to meet you," the older man said.

The two men shook hands, greeting each other warmly.

"And this is Ella," Thea said, gesturing to the little girl.

Ella was nervously attached to Zoe's leg. "Honey, don't be scared. Derek is really nice. I teach him guitar lessons."

"He's really big," Ella whispered.

Derek laughed and crouched down. "Is this better?"

Ella smiled and nodded.

"Hey, have you ever made a flower crown?" Derek asked her, picking a clover off the ground.

"No."

"Well, then I'll make you one. Then you can look like a princess."

Ella loved the sound of that.

"You collect all the clover you can find and bring them to me. Okay?"

"Okay!" Ella scrambled away, searching eagerly for clover.

"You two need to make your rounds," Zoe said. "People are already whispering."

Derek grabbed Thea's hand. "Well, what do you think? Shall we make the rounds?"

Thea looked over her shoulder at the maze of booths and the chattering locals, all eager to know her story. "Yes. Let's do it."

By the end of the day, Derek and Thea were beat. Their voices were raw from telling their story over and over again to the locals, albeit a little bit more PG than the reality.

"We hated each other. And then we didn't," was Thea's line.

To which Derek added, "I actually had a crush on her the whole time, but—"

"He didn't act like it."

They dragged themselves sluggishly into Derek's house—sun-kissed and exhausted—and collapsed on the couch.

It was as if no time had passed. Their bodies twisted into one another's, clutching each other. "Mm, don't let go, okay?" Thea said.

"Never, baby," Derek replied.

Reality, though, was sinking in. They had each other, but neither of them had a job.

"I don't want to be a waitress," Thea grumbled.

"It won't be forever."

"Yeah, but..." She lifted her head. "What was it you were saying the other day?"

"About?"

"About you and me." Thea sat up straighter. "Going into business together."

Derek's heart sang. "Golly, you like to take things fast. What's next? An engagement?"

Thea *thwapped* him on the arm. "You know what I mean. What if we did it?"

He hummed thoughtfully. "I mean, it would take a lot of work."

"It was your idea!"

"I'm not saying I don't want to, I'm just ..." he looked her hard in the eye. "Are you sure you want to do this?"

Thea held out her hand to him. "I want to be your business partner."

Derek took it and shook. "Why is that the sexiest thing you've ever said to me?" He pulled her into his chest and began to kiss her all over her face.

Thea squealed in laughter and soon, they were in a position they knew well, panting and sweaty, arms and legs in a knot, basking in the glow of pleasure no one else had ever given them.

It was risky. But it had been risky since the beginning.

And if Derek had learned anything, it was this: taking a risk for Thea Winton would always pay off.

Chapter Fifteen

THREE MONTHS LATER

November was not yet blanketed with the usual chill. This was good for Thea, who was working in the afternoon sun on a Thursday, planting tulip bulbs in the Kahns' yard.

"Could I have a few reds and yellows?" Thea asked, peering around the base of the oak tree where she was planting.

Derek looked up and raised an eyebrow. "Ketchup and mustard?"

She frowned. "Well, when you put it like that, I guess I don't want them."

He laughed. "How about yellow and purple?" He tossed her a bag of bulbs.

"Thanks." Thea used a trowel to dig up the cold, hardening ground, then popped the bulbs in.

BY DESIGN   127

The Khans were their newest client. Mostly, Thea and Derek had been doing fall yard cleaning and preparing yards for winter. It wasn't the creative work she wanted to do, but it was a start. In only three months, news of Derek and Thea's business, Prairieland Care and Design, had spread like wildfire through Cloverton. Citizens were thrilled to be able to support a local business rather than the Quad Cities transplant. Also, Prairieland's rates were more reasonable, and they'd do smaller jobs. Tate's Landscaping was nearly run out of town.

Though it was only the two of them, and occasionally Hamilton or Rita when they could afford to hire them, their hands seemed to make light work. Thea and Derek were a well-oiled machine. Though building a relationship and a business simultaneously had its downs, most of the time, it was ups.

Their communication was what made their work soar above and beyond. They could get things done efficiently, without too much butting heads, and problem-solve in a pinch.

All that was to say, their relationship only made their work stronger. *Take that, Tim Tate.*

When the Kahns called Prairieland to get their garden in shape to bloom as soon as the frost melted, Derek and Thea leaped at the chance. They'd done all the nitty gritty; fertilizing, laying mulch, preparing for snow. Now, they were able to do bits of design that would make the Kahn's yard bursting with flowers.

"I'm almost done over here," Derek said.

Thea checked her watch. Nearly five. Perfect timing. "Yeah. Me too." Thea tamped down the last bit of earth over her bulbs and got to her feet. "God, I'm beat."

"Gotta get that second wind, babe." Derek popped out from the other side of the tree and smiled. "Hey, Mother Nature."

Thea frowned in confusion. "What?"

He reached out and ran his fingers through her curls, producing a crackly leaf from her hair. "You're taking work home with you."

Thea laughed. "Yeah, that's not good. Need a work-life balance."

Derek grinned. "What's that?"

"How are you two doing out there?" Tracey Kahn called out, poking her head out of the front door.

"Good, Mrs. Kahn!" Thea called back. "We're finishing up for the day."

Tracey came out, wrapped in a cashmere sweater, smiling at the two of them fondly. "I'm sorry, I couldn't help but watch you two from the window. You're just too darling for words."

Derek and Thea exchanged a shy smile. "Thanks, Mrs. Kahn," Thea replied.

"Here's your check for the day. A little something extra in there since it's your last visit," Tracey explained, handing an envelope to Derek.

"Oh, thank you, but that's not necessary. Really," he said.

Thea wanted to elbow him in the side. They had to take everything they could get this early on.

BY DESIGN   129

"Nonsense. It's almost Thanksgiving. Need a little extra something to get the turkey on the table." Tracey began to step away but then stopped. "I wanted to ask you if you two did winter décor. Richard's getting too old to get on the ladder. I mean, he won't say that, but ..." Tracey chuckled, rolling her eyes.

Derek and Thea looked at each other. "We can definitely do that for you, Mrs. Kahn," Thea answered.

"Oh goody," Tracey clapped her hands together. "Well, you two have a relaxing night. And I'll be in touch for the Christmas decorations after Thanksgiving."

As Tracey walked away, Derek sighed. "Thea, I've never hung Christmas lights."

"Me either," she replied. "First time for everything, right?"

He shook his head. "You're a pain in my ass."

She grinned. "You love that about me."

He beamed. "I love everything about you, Thea. Everything."

"And I love everything about you." Leaning into him, she kissed him sweetly.

Going Home

Since Dean Gorman hadn't been back to Cloverton in twelve years, going straight to the old mill as soon as he returned seemed fitting. Like many local teens back in the day, he had worked in the office until he turned eighteen and was legally allowed to be on the floor. However, unlike many of the locals, Dean had decided to move on to greener pastures. After two days of tasting sawdust, he packed his camera and left Cloverton in the rearview.

And he didn't look back.

Though Dean had regrets about how he left, he didn't regret leaving. What he left behind, though... He'd never gotten over that.

He didn't know the mill had closed until a year after the fact. That's when the nightmares began. For nearly a month straight, Dean dreamed of the mill. He dreamed of chaos, fires, and accidents, none of which had happened during his tenure there.

Still, the mill haunted him.

Which was why he had to come back.

Between assignments as a freelance photojournalist, Dean always had his own projects, and this one had been years in the making. He'd spent a summer documenting behind the scenes of county fairs across the country, slept on the ground for weeks while highlighting the experiences of an unhoused person, and had hiked through the Alaskan wilderness with Innuit women searching for a missing daughter.

In the back of his mind, though, he'd always wanted to return to Cloverton and see what had happened to the mill, and consequently the town. He'd seen this scenario a hundred times in his travels. Knowing Cloverton had succumbed to a similar fate made his heart ache. He needed a way to process what had happened to his hometown. That's how the *Defunct Americans* project began. Dean had been traveling the country on his motorcycle shooting shuttered factories and dilapidated towns to highlight the growing invisibility of blue-collar America.

Through his explorations, he'd made many friends, taken thousands of photographs, and now, it was time for the capstone of it all.

Cloverton Lumber.

Dean pulled into the oversize vacant parking lot as dusk settled on a balmy July evening. The building looked more hulking than ever. Sprawling and gray.

He got off his bike and wiped his face with his T-shirt. It'd been a while since he had been in Illinois in the summer. For some reason, the Midwest heat always felt brutal.

Putting a hand to his forehead to block some of the direct sunlight, he stared off in the distance. If he had continued along the road, he would have ended up right in the heart of town. Main Street. He couldn't help but wonder, was the square still the same? Were the stores still open?

He'd driven past the Schnyder's hotel on his way in. It looked even more rundown than it had when he'd left town.

It would break his heart if Cloverton was suffering like so many of the other towns he'd traipsed through over the past month and a half.

For that reason, he decided he wouldn't be making any visits to old haunts or old friends.

Even if there were people he had wondered about.

His parents had retired to Arizona after the mill closed. They had no reason to stick around. Which meant Dean had no reason to visit. None that he would admit to any-way.

He had ignored the genesis of social media almost to a fault. Once a month he sent photos to his assistant who managed to do whatever she needed to do to keep his brand doing whatever it was people did online.

But staying off social media was, what he believed, a testament to his work. It kept it fresh, grounded, nostalgic even.

He had a simple website that he let his agent run. And that was good enough for him.

The tradeoff, though, was not knowing where the people he cared about had ended up all these years since he left. He missed them. He missed the connections from his childhood. But he wasn't sure he was ready to face the past that had broken his heart.

"Three days. That's all," he muttered to himself, retrieving his rucksack from the back of his bike.

Three days to explore the grounds, get all the photos he needed, and then be out of there. He'd have to find a place in one of the buildings to hide the bike to avoid any suspicion from local police.

Before going inside, Dean snapped a quick photo of Cloverton bathed in swaths of orange sunset. That would be a good one to have to show the symbolism of the end of what was.

Dean knew the mill like the back of his hand, and, consequently, knew how to get inside with the least amount of effort or risk of being seen. He ignored all the caution tape and the signs that suggested he'd be prosecuted for trespassing and made his way to the administrative entrance at the top of a white metal staircase that looked so rusty one would think the mill had been closed for ten years instead of five.

He could have contacted the city and gotten a permit. Perhaps even gotten a tour. But the fewer people who knew he was in town, the better.

With a little tinkering of the lock and a few forceful pushes of his shoulder, Dean gained access to the mill.

It was deathly quiet inside. Every step he took echoed through the wide halls.

According to the research he'd done, all the equipment had been sold. All that was left were the offices and gangways above the sawmill floor.

Orange light streamed through the open ceiling, casting a glow over graffiti and debris probably left by local teens and transients. The sight made Dean smile. The abandoned building was like all the others he'd highlighted.

"Now to make camp," he said to himself.

Officer Melanie Hart lowered her head at the sound of approaching footsteps. Determined to stay out of the line of fire, she focused on the paperwork she was filling out on her computer as Chief Wilkes neared her desk.

"Hudson!"

Fellow police officer Chet Hudson looked up from his desk which was adjacent to Mel's.

"I want you to take a walk around the mill when you get a few. Someone reported movement out there."

The caution tape and warning signs were a laughable attempt at staving off local riffraff. The main door had a combination lock box that held the keys. Every police officer and rescue worker had the code, and a few of the riffraff had probably figured it out as well.

What the mill really needed was ongoing surveillance but no one, not even the city, was willing to put money into that effort. If Mel was in charge, she'd pay to have it bulldozed before someone got hurt out there. The temptation of a big empty warehouse was too much to resist for a lot of the youth in town. Exploring the old mill was practically a rite of passage for area teens.

"Someone said there was a guy on a motorcycle outside."

Mel stopped typing. For some reason, the hair on the back of her neck stood on end. "What kind of motorcycle?"

"I don't know. They didn't get a close look."

Mel swallowed and shook her head. *Plenty of people own motorcycles.*

"Give it a once over, would you?"

Chet nodded. "Sure thing."

"Great. Hart," Wilkes said as she walked away with a nod toward Mel.

Mel smiled at the chief before returning to her work. Out of the corner of her eye, she spotted Chet about to open his mouth to talk to her. "Don't even think about asking. I've got paperwork to catch up on."

Chet collapsed back in his chair. "How do you do that?"

"Got two kids. That'll give you a third eye fast."

Chet chuckled. "One doesn't count for anything?"

"Oh, hell no. You need two of them to cause real mischief."

"Erik causes plenty of mischief on his own."

Mel laughed. "Erik is the sweetest kid, and you know it."

"That's why you always gotta be on your toes. You never know when he's gonna turn on you." They both laughed for a moment before Chet picked up where he left off.

"Come on, Mel. I hate that place. It creeps me out. I need backup."

"And I need to do my paperwork."

"Sure you do."

Mel glared at him. It was a fond sort of glare. Chet and Mel had been partners on cases and beats more times than she could count. They were fast friends from the moment Mel joined the force. That was a bonus in a coworker because he didn't tell on her when she waited until the last minute to do paperwork.

She minimized the form she was filling out and started reading the webpage before her.She'd been on the *Net Stars Soccer Camp* site nearly twenty times, intending to enroll her two girls, Hannah and Ellie, before school had even ended. However, every time she did, she couldn't stop staring at the price tag.

The camp had already given her a deal since she was enrolling two children instead of one, but that barely skimmed the surface of the money Mel would have to pull together for soccer camp.

Next, she pulled up a spreadsheet titled *July Budget* and started scrolling through.

What else can I cut back on?

Every month was like this. She couldn't skimp on groceries or gas or the mortgage or utilities. That didn't leave much to play around with when she had two mouths to feed, not including hers.

Fucking Mark.

Mel had that thought at least three times a day for the last five years. Sometimes while doing something as simple as brushing her teeth. Other times while pulling her credit card out at the grocery store. And sometimes, she cursed her ex-husband simply for fun.

Mark had skipped town soon after the mill closed. He lost his job, and his marbles went with it. They'd gotten married right out of high school with Ellie already on the way and, while it wasn't a perfect marriage, Mel had thought it was serviceable. Survivable.

Mark, on the other hand, decided to cut and run to go *find* himself.

She had been heartbroken at first. Now she was pissed off.

But in moments like this, where she was desperate to scrape together the money to register her girls into soccer camp, it hurt. Mel had long been over Mark leaving her, but she still didn't understand how he could leave his children without so much as a goodbye.

Mel hadn't heard from him again except through divorce papers, which she signed gratefully. It didn't surprise her that he never paid the court-ordered child support. She'd taken him to court once, but she wasn't ready to go through that again.

She was strong. She could do this.

"I'll buy you coffee," Chet interrupted her silence. "And a pastry," Chet added when she didn't respond. "I know you can't resist a scone."

Damn it. He was right. And in the heat of summer, the office became a humid mess and started to smell like a high school locker room. She could go for an iced latte about now. "Fine. I'll go."

Chet jumped to his feet with a grin. "That's the spirit."

"But I'm only going for the coffee."

"I know. You won't regret it."

Mel scoffed. She wasn't sure about that.

Continue reading by downloading Going Home now!

Also by Haven Saunders with Marci Wilson

Cloverton Romance Series

Turn the Page: Book One
Faked With Love: Book Two
Music of the Heart: Book Three
In Full Bloom: Book Four
Tattered Dreams: Book Five
By Design: Book Six

We would love to hear from you!

Haven Saunders:
Facebook Author Page: https://www.facebook.com/HavenSaundersAuthor
Facebook Profile: https://www.facebook.com/profile.php?id=100090745508766
Goodreads: https://www.goodreads.com/author/show/29769511.Haven_Saunders
Email: havensaundersauthor@gmail.com

Marci Wilson:
Newsletter: https://marciwilson.com/contact
Instagram: https://www.instagram.com/authormarciwilson/
Facebook Author Page: https://www.facebook.com/authorMarciWilson